Hospitality Revenue and Finance Management

HOSPITALITY REVENUE AND FINANCE MANAGEMENT

Jayanti Prakash

CENTRUM PRESS
NEW DELHI-110002 (INDIA)

CENTRUM PRESS

H.O.: 4360/4, Ansari Road, Daryaganj,
New Delhi-110002 (India)
Tel: 23278000, 23261597, 23255577, 23286875

B.O.: No. 1015, Ist Main Road, BSK IIIrd Stage,
IIIrd Phase, IIIrd Block, Bengaluru-560085 (INDIA)
Tel: 080-41723429

Email: centrumpress@gmail.com
Visit us at: www.centrumpress.com

Hospitality Revenue and Finance Management

First Edition, 2013

ISBN 978-93-81460-08-5

PRINTED IN INDIA

Printed at Balaji Offset, Delhi.

Contents

Preface

The application of revenue management (RM) will become more strategic and will be supported by increasingly sophisticated technology as it includes more of hotels' income streams. In particular, RM will likely be applied to function space, and may also include such revenue streams as spas, restaurants, and golf courses. As a consequence, the revenue management function will become more central to hotel operations, and will quite likely be a separate department that is under the general manager's supervision. The central, strategic role of RM will require upgraded measurement techniques. Rather than revenue per available room (RevPAR), future revenue management may have a profit-oriented metric, such as gross operating profit per available room (GOPPAR) or total revenue per available room or per available unit of area. Future revenue managers will principally need analytical skills, leadership skills, and communication skills. A formal RM education and negotiation skills would also be useful.

The anticipated strategic transformation of RM has major implications. To begin with, the added complexity and strategic orientation will require revenue managers with both strong analytical skills and strong communication skills. It also raises issues of organizational structure for RM, since revenue managers If RM is to be more strategic and technology-driven, the revenue manager of the future will need to be someone with strong analytical skills, a strategic outlook, and the ability to communicate with multiple stakeholders. This strategic focus will extend beyond rate and occupancy to include gross operating profit (at minimum). Also, since RM will encompass all revenue streams within the hotel, the RM function must be structured to allow the RM process to operate in different departments. As a consequence of the hotel-wide strategic operation of RM, the department should be separate from rooms or sales, and should report directly to the hotel GM.

Respondents stressed the need for RM practitioners to see the big picture and, further, they suggested that placing RM within an existing department might limit the function's necessary perspective. Although the respondents expected RM to become a more central aspect of hotel operations, they also foresee a mix of centralization and decentralization, depending a hotel's size and complexity. Larger properties and hotels with multiple revenue streams will probably require on-site revenue managers (reporting directly to the GM).

On the other hand, RM for smaller hotels could be managed regionally or centrally, again depending on the nature of the operation. Part of the decision about centralization involves the high skill level required for good revenue managers—which may even require outsourcing. Another part of the decision to move the RM function outside the hotel is how to balance local knowledge with technical and strategic expertise. The key here is to ensure that RM decisions which require knowledge of the local market remain on the property, while those which do not can be handled either way, depending on available expertise and company policies.

The aim of this book is to present a core of this subject knowledge that is desirable for students. Every attempt has been made to keep abreast of the advances in the subject and at the same time to include the fundamentals.

—*Author*

1

Inventory Management of Hospitality Sector

Introduction

Businesses and public organizations are increasingly interested in the economic impacts of tourism at national, state, and local levels. One regularly hears claims that tourism supports X jobs in an area or that a festival or special event generated Y million dollars in sales or income in a community. "Multiplier effects" are often cited to capture secondary effects of tourism spending and show the wide range of sectors in a community that may benefit from tourism.

Tourism's economic benefits are touted by the industry for a variety of reasons. Claims of tourism's economic significance give the industry greater respect among the business community, public officials, and the public in general. This often translates into decisions or public policies that are favourable to tourism. Community support is important for tourism, as it is an activity that affects the entire community. Tourism businesses depend extensively on each other as well as on other businesses, government and residents of the local community.

Economic benefits and costs of tourism reach virtually everyone in the region in one way or another. Economic impact analyses provide tangible estimates of these economic interdependencies and a better understanding of the role and importance of tourism in a region's economy.

Tourism activity also involves economic costs, including the direct costs incurred by tourism businesses, government costs for infrastructure to better serve tourists, as well as congestion and related costs borne by individuals in the community. Community decisions over tourism often involve debates between industry proponents touting tourism's economic impacts (benefits) and detractors emphasizing tourism's costs. Sound decisions rest on a balanced and objective assessment of both benefits and costs and an understanding of who benefits from tourism and who pays for it. Tourism's economic impacts are therefore an important consideration in state, regional and community planning and economic development. Economic impacts are also important factors in marketing and management decisions. Communities therefore need to understand the relative importance of tourism to their region, including tourism's contribution to economic activity in the area.

A variety of methods, ranging from pure guesswork to complex mathematical models, are used to estimate tourism's economic impacts. Studies vary extensively in quality and accuracy, as well as which aspects of tourism are included. Technical reports often are filled with economic terms and methods that non-economists do not understand. On the other hand, media coverage of these studies tend to oversimplify and frequently misinterpret the results, leaving decision makers and the general public with a sometimes distorted and incomplete understanding of tourism's economic effects. How can the average person understand these studies sufficiently to separate good studies from bad ones and make informed choices? The purpose of this bulletin is to present a systematic introduction to economic impact concepts and methods. The presentation is written for tourism industry analysts and public officials, who would like to better understand, evaluate, or possibly conduct an economic impact assessment. The bulletin is organized around ten basic questions that either are asked or should be asked about the economic impacts of tourism.

The International Tourist Market

Tourism is a major source of economic revenue for countries all around the world. It sustains 200 million jobs, earns over US

$1.3 billion per day, and is the biggest export earner worldwide (World Tourism Organization). Destinations invest millions of dollars into tourism research to understand their market, their competitive positioning and most importantly, how they can use this knowledge to successfully attract tourists. Yet, on September 11, 2001, everything changed. The tourism industry was dealt a mighty blow as the world reeled in the aftermath of the terrorist attacks in New York. People lacked the confidence to travel, flights were cut back, businesses closed, and jobs were lost. And the effects not only hit the immediate players of the tourism industry, but also resounded across other industries that the tourist dollar would normally support. The severity of this situation was only compounded by the War on Iraq and the existence of the SARS virus in 2003, so much so, that for the first time in over 20 years, international tourism arrivals worldwide suffered a negative growth of 0.6% or 4 million arrivals.

India's Place In World Tourism

Tourism has emerged as an instrument for employment generation, poverty alleviation and sustainable human development. Tourism promotes international understanding and gives support to local handicrafts and cultural activities. It is an important segment of the country's economy, specially in terms of its contribution towards foreign exchange earnings, generation of additional income and creation of employment opportunities. The foreign exchange earnings from tourism during the year 2000 were estimated at about Rs. 14,408 crores with an estimated direct employment of about 15 million, which is about 2.4% of the total labour force of the country. Tourism is the third largest foreign exchange earner for India. The International tourist traffic in the country is estimated to be 2.64 million during the year 2000.

However, according to the World Tourism Organisation (WTO), India's share in world tourism arrivals is only 0.38%, accounting for 0.62% of the world tourist receipts. This indicates that much of the tourist potential is yet to be tapped.

With rapid advances in Science & Technology, tourism has acquired the status of an industry in all industrialised countries. The high influx of foreign tourist traffic has accelerated demand for certain economic production and distribution activities. Tourism has emerged as an industry next in importance only to Information Technology industry in the Services sector. By 2005, the contribution of Tourism to the world economy will be doubled. The economic liberalisation in India and consequent foreign investment opportunities, development of tourist facilities including expansion in air-line services, etc. provide an impetus for a spurt in tourist arrivals as in South Asian regions. Domestic tourism plays a vital role in achieving the national objectives of promoting social and cultural cohesion and national integration. Its contribution to generation of employment is very high. With the increase in income levels and emergence of a powerful middle class, the potential for Sdomestic tourism has grown substantially during the last few years.

In its modern form since the end of the Second World War, tourism has grown into one of the world's largest industries with a growth rate in excess of 5 per cent per annum over the past twenty years.

International tourism flows across frontiers in the year 2000 reached 698 million while receipts from these flows reached US$ 595 billion (including receipts from international transport fares). Estimates prepared by the World Tourism Organization indicate that global domestic tourism flows are at least ten times greater than international tourism flows indicating that there were at least 6,980 million domestic arrivals in 2000. Globally, tourism accounts for 11% of the global GDP and 8% of the world trade employment. In most countries with a large population, domestic tourism is the foundation of a viable and sustainable tourism industry. Much of the growth of global tourism has been generated by domestic tourism, which tends to be more focused On rural destinations.

With a growing interest in the intangible culture of different countries (i.e. lifestyles, cuisine, ceremonies, music, religious beliefs, traditions, customs, and history), there is a strong potential to encourage international tourism to the rural areas as well. India's share of global international tourism at 2.64 million foreign arrivals through its borders in the year 2000 is relatively small in volume (about 0.38 per cent) but almost twice as high in terms of US$ receipts (about 0.69 per cent)

On the other hand, India's share of global domestic tourism is much higher (around 4.6 per cent of estimated global domestic tourism). While the proportion of global US$ receipts from international tourism increased from 0.57 per cent in 1990 to 0.69 per cent in 2000, this compares with a share of 1.37 per cent in 1981. In contrast, India's neighbours in South and South-East Asia have more effectively utilised tourism for economic growth and employment creation. A forecasting study undertaken by the World Tourism and Travel Council estimated that in 2001, tourism would account for 10.7 per cent of global Gross Domestic Product, 207.1 million jobs; US$ 1,063.8 billion in export value, and US$ 657.7 billion in capital investment. A study on the economic impact of tourism conducted by the World Tourism and Travel Council estimated that in 2001, the consumption activity arising from domestic and international tourism will contribute 5.3 per cent of India's Gross Domestic Product. Tourism will also sustain 25 million equivalent full time jobs or 6 per cent of India's work force, and contribute more than US$ 3 billion in gross foreign exchange receipts. Separate estimates prepared by the Department of Tourism using a multiplier based on 1980 research suggests that the actual employment generation effect of (direct & indirect) tourism in India is around 42 million (includes full time/part time/casuals). The forecasting study undertaken by the World Tourism and Travel Council further indicates that between 2001 and 2011:-• global Gross Domestic Product will increase from 10.7 per cent to 11 per cent; • global employment contribution will increase from 207.1 million to 260.4 million jobs or 9 per cent of total global employment; • the global value of tourism related exports will increase from US$ 1,063.8 billion to US$ 2,538.3 billion or 12.8 per cent of global export value; and • global capital investment in tourism will increase from US$ 657.7 billion to US$ 1,434 billion or 9.3 per cent of global investment.

The Value of Economic Data

Businesses and public organizations are increasingly interested in the economic impacts of tourism at national, state, and local levels. One regularly hears claims that tourism supports X jobs in an area or that a festival or special event generated Y million dollars in sales or income in a community. "Multiplier effects" are often cited to capture secondary effects of tourism spending and show the wide range of sectors in a community that may benefit from tourism.

Tourism's economic benefits are touted by the industry for a variety of reasons. Claims of tourism's economic significance give the industry greater respect among the business community, public officials, and the public in general. This often translates into decisions or public policies that are favourable to tourism. Community support is important for tourism, as it is an activity that affects the entire community. Tourism businesses depend extensively on each other as well as on other businesses, government and residents of the local community.

Economic benefits and costs of tourism reach virtually everyone in the region in one way or another. Economic impact analyses provide tangible estimates of these economic interdependencies and a better understanding of the role and importance of tourism in a region's economy.

Tourism activity also involves economic costs, including the direct costs incurred by tourism businesses, government costs for infrastructure to better serve tourists, as well as congestion and related costs borne by individuals in the community.

Community decisions over tourism often involve debates between industry proponents touting tourism's economic impacts (benefits) and detractors emphasizing tourism's costs. Sound decisions rest on a balanced and objective assessment of both benefits and costs and an understanding of who benefits from tourism and who pays for it.

Tourism's economic impacts are therefore an important consideration in state, regional and community planning and economic development. Economic impacts are also important factors in marketing and management decisions. Communities therefore need to understand the relative importance of tourism to their region, including tourism's contribution to economic activity in the area.

A variety of methods, ranging from pure guesswork to complex mathematical models, are used to estimate tourism's economic impacts. Studies vary extensively in quality and accuracy, as well as which aspects of tourism are included. Technical reports often are filled with economic terms and methods that non-economists do not understand. On the other hand, media coverage of these studies tend to oversimplify and frequently misinterpret the results, leaving decision makers and the general public with a sometimes distorted and incomplete understanding of tourism's economic effects.

The Economic Impact of Tourism

- *"There are three kinds of lies: damned lies and statistics."*

Why Statistics ?

- "The objective of a national statistical system is to provide relevant, comprehensive, accurate and objective statistical information. Generally, statistics are invaluable for monitoring the country's economic and social conditions, the planning and evaluation of government and private sector programmes and investment, policy debates and advocacy, and the creation and maintenance of an informed public."

Why Statistics ? Cont'd

Essential in:

- Official decision-making, policy formulation
- Policy Analysis & Research
- Academic, business, industrial & other research
- Business planning & CRM
- Citizens/residents being informed about performance of governments

Why Statistics ?

- Facilitate comparison across countries/regions
- Benchmarking
- 'Best Practices'
- Evaluation of performance

However, good statistics must be collected in accordance with agreed international standards using appropriate methods for data collection, processing and dissemination.

Key Tourism Statistics

- Visitor Arrival figures
- Tourism expenditure estimates
- Visitor Surveys (expenditure, motivation, satisfaction etc.)
- Accommodation and Tourism Establishment Surveys
- Tourism Satellite Account (TSA)

Typical tourism experience in regional destination can involve:

- water sports companies, golf clubs
- destination management companies
- yacht charter companies, marine transport companies
- Entertainers
- restaurants, retail outlets, local taxis, tour guides
- telecommunications companies and casinos, etc.

Tourism Measurement Limitations

- In Caribbean absence of a reliable, thorough and internationally uniform statistical database from which one could measure the full economic impact of tourism
- Simple analyses of arrivals, estimates of expenditure (VEMS)
- No in-depth analysis of Tourism economic impact

Tourism Satellite Account

Overview:

- UN SNA '93 recommended TSA
- WTO describes the TSA as the "only way to have an overall view of tourism's impact on the economy on an equal footing with all other sectors."
- Enhance ability to accurately capture economic impact of previously undefined "sectors"

- Analytical work done within existing national accounting systems
- More flexible
- Not overburdening CSNA

Tourism Satellite Account

Uses:

- *Provide credible data on the impact of tourism and related employment*
- *Serve as a standard framework for organizing statistical data on tourism*
- *Become a new internationally accepted national accounting standard endorsed by the UN Statistical Commission*
- *Function as a powerful instrument for designing economic policies related to tourism development*
- *Measure tourism's contribution to GDP and its ranking in relation to other economic sectors*
- *Provide data on tourism's impact on a country's Balance Of Payments*
- *Provide information on tourism human resource characteristics*
- *Measure the level of investment in tourism*
- *Evaluate tax revenues generated by tourism industries*
- *Measure the level of tourism's consumption of other goods and services*

Tourism Satellite Account

Benefits:

- *Reconciliation of the demand-side data with the supply-side data within the account brings greater coherence to the definition of the industry; all partners in the industry will speak a common language.*
- *Use of a recognized accounting system brings enhanced credibility to the economic analysis of the industry.*
- *Use of an accounting framework can bring other important information into the analysis of tourism, such as data on value-*

added benefits of tourism, share of GDP, government revenues, human resources development or financial flows.

Using Surveys to Assess Visitor Expenditure & Motivation, etc.

Uses of Tourism Surveys:

- demand side (visitor satisfaction, motivation, expenditure etc.)
- supply side (quality and standards of tourism establishments, employment, attitudes of residents etc.)
- Travel patterns and expenditure of regional and international visitors

Using Surveys to Assess Visitor Expenditure & Motivation, etc.

Uses of Tourism Surveys cont'd:

1. RM/Visitor comment & feedback
2. Evaluation of tourism promotion programmes

Information collected from surveys used to:

- customize policies and strategies
- redress any supply problems
- enhance the tourism product
- provide more competitive and attractive destination or experience for the visitor.

CTO/CRSTDP Statistics Workshop 2005

Formula for determining Return on Investment from specific spending

- E.g. Tourism Advertising campaign

ROI Formula:

- Inquiries * Conversion rate * length of stay * party size * Avg. spending = Total expenditure
- Total Advertising costs = (Costs of advertisement placement/prod. + website development)

ROI = Total Spending/Advertising costs

E.g. Tourism Advertising campaign

- Inquiries = brochures + website visits
- In this example inquiries = 40,000 brochures+ 15,000 website visits = 55,000 inquiries
- Conversion rate is 25% [gross conversion (# people who came, e.g. 60%) and net conversion (# people who came because of advertising, e.g. 25 %)
- Average length of stay is 6 days
- Average party size is 2.6 people
- Average daily expenditure is $100
- Total Advertising costs = $100,000 (advertisement placement & production)+ $10000 (website development costs) = 110,000

E.g. Tourism Advertising campaign

- Total Spending = 55,000*25%*6 days*2.6 people* $50 per day = $10,725,000
- Therefore Net ROI is: 9,750,000/110,000 = 97.5
- For every advertising dollar spent, the return to the country was $97.50 in traveller spending.

. ourism Statistics in Macro-Economic Planning

- Accurate statistics fundamental to good economic planning !
- Planners use statistical databases, spreadsheets and modern analytical techniques to prepare reports and recommendations for governments etc.
- Analytical techniques utilized to project program costs and forecast future trends in aggregate demand (GDP), employment, housing, investment, taxation, transportation and population

Tourism Statistics in Macro-Economic Planning cont'd

Reliable and timely tourism statistics:

- crucial to projections & forecasting
- vital to better planning of tourism sector and to justify its expansion

- long-term and short-term plans for optimal land use
- decisions on trade-offs between competing uses re: growth maximization

Reliable and timely tourism statistics necessary for rationalizing:

- economic, political and social needs
- traffic congestion, air, water and soil pollution
- effects of growth and change on community *vs* potential benefits from tourism development
- necessary to have reliable data on trends and projections in key sectors, including the tourism sector
- not making best use of community's land and resources can be counterproductive to the particular development
- crucial to policy framework formulation
- informed decision-making by both public and private sectors at international, regional, national and local levels

Policy formulation involves:

- Defining the objectives of tourism development.
- Setting growth targets for tourism.
- Determining the type of tourism to be attracted.
- Defining public and private responsibilities.
- Minimizing deleterious effects of tourism

Economic Impacts

- Direct (first round)
- Indirect (upstream)
- Induced (tourism $ in Dom Y)
- Negative (leakages)
- Positive (government revenues, externalities,multiplier effect)

Tourism Statistics in Business Planning & Investment Decisions

- Rapid growth of tourism necessitate more focused and

informed planning and investment decisions by tourism business

- Given massive investments and lender/shareholder demands tourism growth projections must be rigorous and as accurate as possible
- [e.g. in Turtle territory]

Business planning:

- involves anticipating and controlling change to maximize benefits of tourism
- requires enterprises to rely on statistics for research, planning & design of marketing programs
- needs reliable data for financial projections
- demands industry and sector performance statistics for comparative analyses

Investors

Rely on tourism statistics for:

- decision-making and financing proposals
- evaluating performance/justifying investments
- monitoring implementation of government policies
- building partnerships with airlines, governments etc.
- benchmarking performance of host country vs competing destinations
- policy advocacy in trade associations

Accommodation Surveys

- *Commercial Accommodation Classification Survey in New Zealand*
    * Survey data recorded using particular groupings (classifications) and terms.
- Classifications

Survey provides information on groupings used Commercial Accommodation Survey Includes geographical, establishment and employee type classifications.

Classifications cont'd

- Geographical classifications
- Origin of guests
- Origin of establishments.

The Demand for Tourism

Tourism demand is the foundation on which all tourism-related business decisions ultimately rest. Governments and companies such as airlines, tour operators, hotels, cruise ship lines, and recreation facility providers are interested in the demand for their products by tourists. The success of many businesses depends largely or totally on the state of tourism demand, and ultimate management failure is quite often due to the failure to meet market demand.

One of the most interesting element in the tourism industry is the tourism demand. Demand as the economic concept refers to the amount of the definite products which the consumer is ready to buy, on fixed price, in the particular time and with the pointed circumstances. There is an economic rule: if the price is high, the demand for the product is lower and vice versa. But there are some exception to the rule. In general the are three main principal elements of the tourism demand. They are:

- an effective demand, which contain the amount of people who actually are participating in tourism. The commonly accepted way of measuring the actual demand is the number of travellers;
- a restrained demand, which means the amount of people, who have the desire to travel, but have no possibility to do it because of different circumstances. This type of demand is called the potential demand. If the restricting factors disappear, the potential demand becomes the effective demand;
- a deferred demand, which also can become the actual demand;
- no demand, which is characterized as the absence of desire to travel and to visit different countries.

There also a lot of the other approaches to the tourism demand. For example, the deputizing of demand, which means the substitution one activity connected with tourism for another similar activity. The another view consider the displacement of demand, which refers to the case when the geographical location of tourism interests changes. A very effective way to support and to extend the tourism demand is to open and develop new tourist centres, resorts and places of attraction. The way to attract the wide demand for these new resorts divides into three main approaches:

- to readdress the demand from the similar resorts in the area to the new places of attraction;
- to replace the demand from the absolutely dissimilar resorts to the new;
- to create the new effective demand.

The Tourist's need and Wants

Visitors want their expectations satisfied. Some will be demanding, some not. But most will be very pleased if the bathrooms are clean.

Some travellers are comforted by moving out of their comfort zones and others need substantial hand-holding throughout the journey. In most cases travellers wish to figure out how to interact with locals that is not exploitative.

Visitors have different information demands. Eco travellers want to know where the water comes from, what is growing in the fields. Many are interested in la Earlier studies acknowledged the following key motivation elements in relation to tourism. They are; the need to escape (for example a dreary home life) and to seek (new and exciting experiences). There is still acceptance of the undimentional approach to motivation on the understanding that a variety of behaviours can be explained as a response of a small number of motivational 'needs'. This appears to be the main view despite suggestions that motivation may be out-dated since the decision process is a result of many experiences and knowledge of destinations. suggests that motivation's two dimensions are lasting dispositions and object-specific elements nguage and want to know the names of the trees.

General and Specific Motivation

According to some tourist motivation theories, motivations are developed as a result of 'pull' and 'push' factors. Pull factors relate to the characteristics or attractions of a travel destination. For cultural tourists visiting Australia, they include attractions such as the Sydney Opera House and Aboriginal sites. Push factors relate to the needs and wants of individuals that lead them to 'buy' particular holidays. For cultural tourism and tourism as a whole, they include the desire for social interaction and relaxation, to experience something different and to learn about themselves and the places they visit for participating in cultural activities.

Segmenting the Tourism Market

Market segmentation is essentially the process of dividing the total market into more manageable groups of people with similar buying characteristics. Avoiding a mass market approach means that sales messages can be more targeted and distribution channels tailored to the segments' needs. Segments must be discernible so you can differentiate one segment from another. Each segment also needs to be a reasonable size otherwise it won't be economically viable to target it. You should also have a product, or be able to develop one, that is appropriate to each segment you choose. It's also important to avoid making segments too large because it's much harder to develop suitable promotional messages for larger segments.

If you focus on just a few segments won't you miss out on others? Some tourism providers become concerned that by targeting only a segment of the total market, they will miss out. The reverse is usually true. The aim is to choose a limited number of segments and to understand those markets really well. This means that marketing messages are clearer and stronger. There is a ripple effect as people outside the chosen segments find these stronger messages more appealing and are also attracted to that product.

The following two diagrams demonstrate this. The first box shows the "something for everyone" approach used by many tourism providers. They don't want to exclude any markets so they try to embrace them all. But their marketing efforts and messages are rarely strong enough to reach the people at the centre of their markets so they go untapped. Market segmentation is a method of dividing a large market in to smaller groupings of consumers each having common needs or behaviour. We have two types of markets:

a) Homogenous Market: a market in which people or organisation have similar characteristics

b) Heterogeneous Market: a market in which people or organisations have different characteristics

Market segmentation allows a marketer to take a heterogeneous market and carve it up in to one or more homogenous markets which are made up of individuals or organisations with similar needs, wants and behavioural tendencies. In short, market segmentation in tourism helps in.

a) efficient use of marketing resources to cater to a particular type of tourists,

b) better understanding of customer needs and providing better satisfaction,

c) better understanding of the competitive situation and emerging trends, and

d) achieving accuracy in the measurement of goals and performances.

Market segmentation involves a division of the prospective market into identifiable groups. In simple words, it can be defined as the division of a market into groups of segments having similar wants.

This theory is opposed to the diluting of efforts by appealing to an entire market. It is based on a realisation of the fact that a product can be sold more effectively if efforts are concentrated towards those groups which are most potential.

Philip Kotter is of the view that different "competitors will be in the best position to go after particular segments of the market" and each "organisation, instead of trying to reach every one, should identify the most attractive parts of the market that it could effectively serve". At the same he mentions that this is not always the practise. The organisations, in their thinking about operating in a market have generally passed through the following three stages:

Mass Marketing: This is a marketing style where the organisation makes efforts to attract every eligible buyer to use its product which has been mass produced and will be mass distributed. Here no attention is paid to consumer preferences.

Organisation Product Mass Market

Product Differentiated Marketing: In this marketing style the organisation produces two or more products for the entire market. These products might have different characteristics but they are not designed for any different group(s). Rather they only provide alternatives to every buyer in the market.

Product

Organisation Market (Two Options)

Product

Target Marketing: Here, the organisation:

- differentiates amongst varied market segments,
- focuses on one or more of these segments (targets), and
- develops the product to meet the needs of the target market.

In tourism, the organisations practice each style of marketing though the emphasis on target marketing is gaining ground. Let us take the example of Airlines vis-a-vis the tourist market.

- Under stage-1, airlines are available for everyone to travel.
- Under stage-2, the airlines offer Royal class, J class, Business class, Economy class or one can hire charter flight or a chopper.
- Under stage-3, special airline services to pilgrim both domestic (dhams) or Vaishno Devi or international (Haj, Jerusalem) which have set target of customers from among the up budget tourist market.

This shift of emphasis is because of the benefits in market segmentation.

- By selecting the market niches, i.e., suitable markets, an organisation can exploit the market much better.
- An organisation can focus its strategies more appropriately on target groups.

Segmentation and Targetting Approaches in Tourism

It is true that product can be sold more effectively if efforts are concentrated towards those groups which are most potential. In the words of Philip Kotler, "Competitors will be in the best position to go after particular segments of the markets and each organisation instead of trying to reach everyone, should identify the most attractive parts of market that it would effectively serve". He also acknowledges that in practice marketers operating in the markets have generally passed through following three stages:

Mass Marketing

- Efforts are made to attract every eligible buyers
- No attention is paid to consumer preferences, e.g., airline for every one who can afford, same by all airlines.

Target Marketing

- Varied segments are differentiated
- Focus on one or two of these segments
- Products are developed to meet their needs, e.g., operating of short/shuttle services between popular business destinations for corporate travellers or for pilgrims. For international pilgrimages, Haj, etc. and for domestic, Vaishnodevi, Kedarnath, Ajmer, Neelkanth, etc.

Product Differentiated Segmentation

- Organisation produces two or more products for entire market but produces specialised products for particular groups
- Only to provide alternatives to every buyer in the market, e.g., an airline offering different classes. "J" class, "Y" class, Royal Class, etc. Some airlines provide more leg and luggage space according to their class of journey.
- the product matches the needs of that segment.

The purpose of market segmentation in tourism marketing is to:

- Segment the markets generating tourists, and
- Identify the prospective tourists according to lifestyles, socio-economic status, attitudes about travel, etc.

This is done to best qualify these tourists for high prospect customer status. This high potential prospect is defined in terms of how closely his/her vacation preferences and lifestyles match up to what the destination has to offer. In other words, the purpose is to go for cost-effective marketing. This can be achieved by designing, promoting and delivering the tourism products or services in such ways that the identical needs of the target groups are satisfied. A crucial aspect here is what is grouped in forming market segments. Consumers are not mutually exclusive categories and what is grouped together is the customers' probability of purchasing different types of product offers. Hence, it is necessary to understand what is wanted and who is going to buy it. A marketing person has to gain knowledge about this and he or she can approach this problem by asking certain questions like:

What

- factors influence the tourist demand?
- services do the tourists expect?
- is the basis for tourists comparing your product with other products?
- benefits do the tourists seek?
- risks do the tourists perceive?
- are the tastes of the tourist?

How

- do tourists buy?
- much are the tourists willing to spend?
- many vacations do the tourists take in a year?
- does promotion and advertising effect the tourists' demand?
- does the product fit into the life styles of tourists?

Where

- is the decision made by tourists to buy?
- do the tourists seek information about the product?
- do the tourists buy the product?

When

- do the tourists take a vacation?
- do the tourists make a decision to buy the product?
- is the product repurchased?

Why

- do the tourists buy your product?
- do the tourists choose one destination over the other?
- do the tourists go to a particular destination?
- do the tourists prefer one type of service and not the other?
- do the tourists buy your competitors' products?

Who

- buys your product?
- buys your competitors' products?
- are likely to buy your product?
- may not be interested in your product?

You must remember here that this list of questions is only suggestive and the nature of questions will depend on the nature of your product and certain specific situations. Besides, you will need the back up data and information for finding answers to these questions which may not always be possible. But you should not be discouraged by the limitations. Depending upon the study's purpose, various approaches are employed in the tourism industry to identify market segments. Segments can be defined either by descriptive or casual factors. Descriptive factors simply describe the characteristics of the person found in a segment. The "why" of a person's action, however, is better obtained through additional use of causal factor information which identifies the motivation behind a decision. A practical and Actionable Segmentation requires profiling of both:

- Past visitors, and
- Prospective visitors.

This is done to ensure proper matches and to determine the actual size of each high potential segment, in terms of:

- Geographics,
- Deomgraphics
- Psychographics, and
- Travel Habits.

In other words, we can say that the:

Target for Marketing = Characteristics + Demographic profile of Consumers, Products and Services)

The studies of marketing experts like Kotler and Chisnall show that in order to make any segment actionable for marketing, each segment must be:

1) Discrete, i.e., the separate identity of the sub-group must be established by using any criteria like income, purpose, interest, etc.
2) Measurable, i.e., the characteristics that distinguish the sub-groups should be measurable through the available data.
3) Viable, i.e., the projected earnings to be achieved should be more than the costs of designing the market mix.
4) Appropriate, i.e., showing the inseparability of the tourism product which should contribute to the overall image in the market.

Segmentation Factors

In practice, the ground for tourism market segmentation shall be, of course, on the basis of:

a) Geographic factors: Since tourism involves movement of millions of people across the international boundaries, it is an acknowledged fact that the tourists' needs differ according to geographic regions. For instance, tourist coming from Australasia region would have altogether different needs than a tourist coming from North America. Not only this even tourists coming from two different coasts of America have different needs, desires and attitudes. Therefore, to market successfully your product or services you must understand varied needs of the tourists coming from different geographic areas. It is only then that you can categorise your potential segments in a homogenous manner. Therefore, it is advisable that you should try to target a segment for your product which lacks that particular product/service you are marketing. For instance, you sell deserts of Rajasthan to tourists from Germany, UK or France which have no deserts. Similarly, if you are trying to sell your mountain based activities to tourist from countries who do not have such snow capped peaks. You may succeed but if you try to target tourist from Switzerland or Austria you cannot succeed. On the same pattern don't try to sell your coastal beauties to tourist from Australasia or Pacific but try to sell them to tourists who don't have such coastal attractions in their countries. Kerala started marketing "monsoon tourism to tourists from Middle East" but the same cannot be sold to tourists from North-East India. Here Kerala will have to sell beaches and back waters.

b) Demographic Profiles: This factor is a vital factor for developing tourism products and services. It means to segment your product service market on basis of income, age, sex, family size, lifestyle, family life cycle, education, religion, race and nationality and so on. If you fail to design your product or segment your market without giving due consideration to these factors then there may be serious repercussions for your product or service. It is important because:

   i) Consumer wants, preferences and usage rates are associated with demographic variables, and

   ii) this method is easy in measurement and interpretation of data.

For instance, India being a long haul destination (average length of stay is 27.2 days) and our major markets are America, Europe, Far East and Australasia. The demographic profile of these markets will help in marketing decision making. If we look at the demographic characteristics of the European market, we see:

Age: between 25 – 59 years

Sex: majority of males, alone females very few

Family sizes: 2 – 4 members

Family Life Cycle: single/married without children (DINKS) or with children below the age of 14.

Income: Euro 7000 and above

Occupation: professionals, executives, teachers and professors

Education: Higher secondary and above

Nationality: German, French, Italia, Swiss, Dutch, Spanish and Swedes

Based on this data a marketer can develop, rejuvenate or alter his or her tourism products.

c) Psychographic Grounds: Division of groups on the basis of their social status, life styles and/or personality characteristics is very essential in tourism marketing. While using demographic parameters of income, we can divide the target segment in to upper middle class, middle class and lower middle class. Each of these sub-variable will have different tastes, likings, status, product preferences, etc. accordingly. Personality characteristics also play and important role in product development and market segmentation. For instance, if you are targeting at tourists for adventure sports related tourism, their real market segment would be tough and strong or adventure seekers only. These people shall be young and so would naturally belong to low budget or lower income.

* Another important criteria for segmenting the tourist market is on the basis of personality traits, i.e., some members of potential targeted market are allocentrics.

Money wouldn't be a constraint for this segment but they want to visit a new and adventurous place every time. They don't like to repeat the same destination. They love to be called first timers or trendsetters to be followed by the masses (psycocentrics) who have a fear for unknown and who want to perform repeat visits.

* In this category, as a marketer, you should also try to identify those who are self made, successful socialite, mainstreamers, aspirers or innovator type of people because they are the ones who are most likely to purchase tours to far away countries.
* It is also advisable that you should try to segment your market with an idea that among certain categories of tourists there can be found some common attitudes. For example, people in the age group of 18-26, want to have vacation full of leisure and thrill, while others who look for adventure can form another group.

d) Behavioural Grounds: In psychological terms the whole range of generation of wants and their transformation in to buying or using decisions can be explained as behaviour. Before learning about transformation process of attitudes of tourists in to action we should know who are users and what is their base:

Foreign Tourist, Domestic Tourist, Youths, Students, Executives, Artists, Politicians, Academicians, Pilgrims, Representatives, Sportsmen

* General Classification
* Sex as a base
* Male, Female
* Region as a base
* Urban, Rural, Cosmopolitan, Sub urban
* Education as a base

Professional, Worker, Vocational, Artists, Professor, Craftsmen, business man, etc.

* Status as a base
* Upmarket, Budget Market, Low-Class Market
* Occupation as a base
* White Collar or Blue Collar Tourist

In view of this, the marketing decision cannot be sound unless the marketers make an in-depth study of the visitors' behaviour with focussed attention on customer satisfaction.

Before arriving at sound marketing decisions, the marketers are required to see that users are aware or unaware; interested or intend to purchase either on trial or experimental basis; whether user is light user (non-frequent) or heavy user (frequent users),.

This kind of study will help the marketers to focus their advertisements on the service sensitivity of the users. In tourism market segmentation a large number of behaviouristic variables are used. Among important ones a few are:

I) Occasion for travel: You can segment your tourist market on the basis of the occasion they use for travelling. For instance, you can segment your tourist markets as business tourist market, holiday/leisure market, VFR (visiting Friends and Relations) market, adventure tourist market, heritage tourism market, or honeymooners market and so on so forth.

II) Benefit derivation: Segmentation on the basis of benefits identifies the:

   i) major benefits that the customer looks for in the product;

   ii) kind of people who look for each benefit; and

   iii) major brands that deliver each benefit.

According to Kotler many products are made-up of three "core benefit segments",

i) quality buyers – more concerned with product image rather than cost;

ii) service buyers – product that provides good service, i.e., best value for money; and

iii) economy buyers – who are more concerned with the cost and, therefore, would like to keep it low.

Kotler further classifies customers on the basis of behaviouristic attitudes in to four categories on the basis of behaviouristic attitudes:

i) hard-core loyals – would never think of switching over;

ii) soft-core loyals – may think of one or two alternatives;

iii) shifting loyals – gradually favour one product/organisation over other; and

iv) switchers – those who have no loyalty to any organisation.

Kotler's this classification of customers is very useful form the perspective that you can pin-point which brands are most competitive to you. By knowing the product and market strategies of your competitor you can successfully convert your soft core loyals customers in to hardcore customers by offering them incentives like free mileage or free accommodation when they accumulate required mileage or number of nights.

III) Associated characteristics: Besides the benefits sought by tourists, you can also use other associated characteristic for segmenting your market. These are:

i) User status: In this category a tourist may be segmented as first time visitor or repeat visitor, past-visitor or potential visitor, etc.

ii) Usage rage: This can be illustrated as frequent usage called frequent fliers for an airline or for hotels ex-numbers of night spent to earn points for complimentary services.

iii) Loyalty status: This highlights the loyalty of your customer who remains loyal to you in spite of many allurements to shift to other products or service. Therefore, your company must study its own hardcore loyals and devise marketing strategies to maintain their loyalty. For example, an airline offers members of its frequent fliers scheme, quick check-in or extra baggage allowances, priority in confirmation of seats or special waiting lounge.

IV) Buyer-readiness stage: This is a crucial factor for market segmentation since an in-depth study of this allows marketers to launch their product at right time. For example, if you decide to launch special packages for all family members, readiness stage would be when all the members have leisure, i.e., when they have a vacation. In another example, private domestic airlines started their services when they realised that domestic air travellers were weary of monopolistic attitude of the national carrier.

V) Attitudes: No doubt tourism market can be classified by the degree of enthusiasm tourist or a potential tourist shows in buying a destination. Keeping in view this you may encounter tourists who are enthusiastic, positive, indifferent or hostile in their attitude towards the destination. It would be easier for you to sell a destination to those who are enthusiastic and positive in their attitude.

Price factor: By now you must have gathered a fair idea that tourism market constitutes of:

i) those who are high spenders and are prepared to pay high prices and they are described as up-budget tourists;

ii) those who want to take low priced vacation; and

iii) those who may take a moderately priced holiday.

It is true that price range communicates to consumers the quality expectations of a product along with the producer's image. Today destinations in South Eat Asia are cheaper than travelling within India. For example, Bangkok is being sold at $25 per night, Singapore at $40 per night, etc. This is able to attract large volume of outbound tourism from India.

Other Variables

Tourism markets are also segmented on the basis of travelling habits of tourists, which include:

a) Distance Travelled: Whether potential tourist segment belongs to long haul, short haul or mid haul tourist. This is classified on the basis of the distance a tourist travels. For India, tourists from Europe, Far East or USA are long haul market segments whereas Nepal or Bangladesh are short haul.

b) Duration of Trip: Segmentation of tourist markets can also take place on basis of short-break holidays of 2-3 days or long trips of 20 or more days for instance to USA or Europe.

c) Time of Travel: Tourist markets can also be segmented on the basis of time period when they travel. For example some tourists prefer to travel during summer holidays while some prefer to travel during winter holidays or some take a holiday in both summer and winter. In Europe, normally, longer trips are taken during summer seasons, since vacation is longer in summer than winters.

d) Organisation of Trips: Marketers also segment the market on the basis of how do they travel, i.e., whether they travel individually (FIT) or in groups (GITS). On the other hand, some of your customers will buy only air tickets or in some cases only hotel bookings will be sought.

e) Religion as Travel Motive: Since ancient times man has travelled for religion motives be it to have a holy dip in the revered rivers or to visit any temples devoted to their deities or even for the sake of visiting religious fairs or melas. Undoubtedly religion has always been one of the prime motive for travel. However, in present times specialise services are prepared and delivered to this niche market whether they are Muslim tourists; Hindus (Dhamyatra) or Christians. You must have noticed that there is a particular time for each of there segments to travel. For instance, Haj travellers travel between the month of January and March; Hindu tourists visit their dhams or other religious shrines like Vaishno Devi, Shirdi, Kalka, etc. during summer vacations, i.e., May to July; and, of course, Christians travel during October and December.

Motivators and Facilitators

Travel motive is an inner force which create a desire in a person to travel. Motivating factors will vary from one person to another. This unit is aimed at imparting the knowledge and understanding among learner regarding the classification of travel motivations.

1. *Physical motivators:* Physical motives are the factors which helps to improve the physical and mental well being of individuals.
2. *Cultural motivators:* Cultural motivators are factors like music, dance, architecture, folk lore, arts and crafts, customs etc. which attracts tourists to a particular destination.
3. *Interpersonal motivators:* Interpersonal motivators are the factors which create desire to visit relatives and friends, meet new people, establish new friendships etc. It also includes ethnic motives and family reasons.
4. *Status and prestige:* Some people undertake travel because they think it is fashionable. Status and prestige motivators include motives related to business and profession.

Factors Influencing Changes in Tourism Demand

Tourism has to face a challenging change in its framework conditions: The geopolitical as well as the economic situation require new strategies. Technological innovations, demographic change and a powerful costumer have to be met in politics, marketing and planning. New destinations, new products with prices on a level, which would have been incredible some years ago, compete with the established tourism offer.

We may look at the "New Demand Factors" from two perspectives. On the one hand we have those factors influencing the demand, i.e. the motivation to travel and the ability to travel, directly or indirectly. They cover a wide range from the general economic situation, over politics to technological innovations, just to name some examples. On the other hand we have emerging factors, i.e. the changing face of consumer behaviour in tourism like destinations preferences, quality expectations, booking behaviour etc. But what the tourist does can not only be explained by external factors alone. The experienced and educated traveller will change his behaviour even in a constant framework. Thus, there is an endogenous dynamic within the tourist behaviour. The emerging (from external and endogenous factors) patterns characterize the tourism consumers and their behaviour within the next years.

The Situation

Holiday travel does not generally mean international travel. In most European countries domestic travel exceeds the international holiday trips. Of course, there are some exceptions like Germany or the Netherlands or – quite naturally-small countries like Luxembourg.

The total volume of European tourism demand has been quite stable, but the structure underneath showed quite a dynamic.

Vacations are not only for the fun of the travellers: Holiday tourism has become an important economic sector, a social achievement, a political Instrument, and an educational tool.

Influencing Factors

As we all experience the change around us the questions arises how these developments will have an impact on tourism demand. To name just a few categories:

- Economy
- Politics
- Crisis and threats
- Demographic Change
- Technology

In addition we have to take into account the influences coming from general changes in consumer attitudes and, finally, the tourism industry itself, of course influencing the demand side of tourism (e.g. standardization of products, information channels, (over) capacities and price strategies).

* All these factors are linked to each other.
* How can these factors have an impact?
* Holiday demand is driven by needs, motives, and expectations, its realization depends on the individual economic situation and the freedom to travel.

Thus:

- External factors may have an impact on tourism demand by affecting the *ability* to travel (freedom, time, money, fitness) and the *motivation* to do so.
- Consumer Behaviour is not a reaction on a single factor but on the whole *set of influencing external factors*. In addition it is driven by internal factors (e.g. motives, abilities etc.). Thus, the impact of a change in a single external factor is limited.

Most of the external factors seem to be *in favour for a sound development* of tourism demand in Europe in the years to come. However, there are no signs for a general boom.

Emerging Factors

As we can't limit our attention to a single external factor and its impacts, we look at several of the emerging factors, new trends in tourism emerging from the whole set of influences and the endogenous dynamics of tourism. These emerging trends will not change tourism over night. Trend research has shown that the future developments will most probably come as a step-by-step development, not as a revolution. Giving the global and nearly unlimited offer in tourism with capacities still on the rise at least in Europe the power in the market is clearly with the consumer. He will only choose products which fit into his motivation and expectations. Taking the efforts to reduce seasonality in tourism as an example, we clearly see that the limitations to these efforts are only partly due to e.g. school holiday regulations but predominantly due to the motivation of spending a holiday under nice weather conditions.

New Source Markets

The enlargement of the European Union in 2004 and 2007 sure is important for the whole continent. Poland, Hungary, the Czech Republic, Estonia, Latvia, Lithuania, Slovenia, Slovakia, Malta and Cyprus have joined the European Union on May 1, 2004. The EU since then embraces 25 countries. The size of the EU has grown by 25%, the population by 20%, the GDP by 5%. However, its short time effects on tourism are limited. But the general political process, under way since some 20 years, which the EU enlargement is a "natural" part of, contribute a lot to a changing tourism demand in Europe.

As destinations, the new EU-members benefit from a bonus this year: The extensive coverage in the media will influence the growing interest in these countries and the felt distances will decrease. However, for most holiday makers, almost the whole world is accessible for a vacation. For holiday destinations this means a continuously growing competition-a competition in which the new EU-member countries will have to participate as well: No guarantee for success for anybody, but chances for everybody! The dynamic in holiday tourism is based on continuous, long-term developments, not in sudden changes.

Naturally there are not only potentials and chances, but also barriers preventing a fast development in tourism. Experts mention the following reasons for Eastern Europe: Low investment rates, undeveloped traffic system, undeveloped infrastructure in the countryside, unsatisfactory quality of hotels and gastronomy, weaknesses in tourism marketing. Of course this does not go for every single destination. There are also limits on the demand side. Images are playing an important role when deciding upon a holiday destination. Closely connected to images are holiday motives. People choose holiday destinations mainly based on their suitability of fulfilling their holiday motives. Political settings or changes, like the EU-enlargement, are comparatively nimportant.

To raise the demand for the new EU-member countries, (potential) holiday makers must be convinced that their holiday motives can very well (or better) be fulfilled in these countries. Now is the time for a powerful marketing. People are going to make use of their new freedom and the opportunities connected to rising welfare (at least those, who participate in the economic upswing).

Demographic Change

Demographic change is a constant process but has got a lot of public attention in recent years. These are major demographic changes that are already influencing society today and that are worth a closer look on how they may have an impact on holiday travel behaviour. Examples for other important demographic trends are: Rising educational level, a more colourful society due to migration, a changing role of women in society. Research has shown that people do not change their travel behaviour just because they turn 60 or 65, or because they retire. In most cases they stick to the holiday patterns acquired till the middle of their life. This fact allows for predictions of the tourist behaviour of future senior generations: within 15 years the number of holiday tourists in the age group 70 to 80 years to rise by more than 50% (from 4,2 mn. in 2003 to 6,6 mn. in 2018) with more than 2/3 choosing a destination abroad (today: 50%; 2003 figures from RA 2004). Less dramatic are the changes in the segment of *family holidays*: Taking again Germany as an example: The number and share of Holiday trips with children (up to 13 years) has proved to be stable in Germany for more than a decade with some 22% of all holiday trips. In 2003 this share resulted in 14.4 mn holiday trips. With an 8%.

Information Search and Travel Decisions: Skilled Consumers with Low Involvement

Along with this structural developments the consumer behaviour changes as well. One of the important fields is in the pre-trip phase the search for information and the way a decision for a certain tourist product is made. The immense tourism offer available able to fulfil the individual needs leads the way to *interchangeable products*. For the consumer it doesn't make much of a difference whether travelling to destination A or B, with the tour operator X or Y etc. Actually, with all the communication channels and the more and more detailed information available the consumer is in a state of *information overload*. Impossible to consider everything!

Thus, the holiday decision is not the final result of a comprehensive search-evaluate-choice process but a *good-enough solution* considering a few aspects of a few products (those being in the relevant set) from a few information sources. Rational arguments are not very important. This is the state consumer researcher call "*low involvement*". With basic needs fulfilled and low involvement conditions *convenience* (taking the easy way) and *experience* orientation together with *variety seeking* are getting more important. Naturally, there is nothing new about experience orientation in tourism.

Consumers' Paradox: Meet the Standards & be Different

With globalization of the tourism industry, a computer based distribution, and the strive to offer high quality, *standardization* of tourism products is a must. That constitutes a risk for tourism because "standard" is nothing offering new experiences or meeting the trend for variety seeking. At the same time the tourism demand and the products get more and more *differentiated* and fragmentized, e.g. with winter sports, study trips or family holidays. The consumer expects both: *quality* and *difference.*

Standardization and *differentiation* are main trends of both the consumers' and the industry's side. Again, this is an additional challenge for the industry, because this means more efforts necessary without a growing demand or even a growing turn-over.

Conclusions

Looking at the mayor trends we can summarize:

- High volume of tourism demand around Europe with a few growth potentials in some source markets.
- Source markets are different: from *close to saturated* to *offering growth potentials* and need specific treatment in marketing.
- General market conditions, skilled consumer and vast capacities in tourism are a challenge for tourism marketing, especially in the big close to saturated markets.

But holiday tourism has manifold functions. It is an economic sector (for both destinations and the travel industry), a social achievement, a political Instrument, and an educational tool. Different sectors see tourism as a tool for different objectives. The evaluation of the situation and the future perspectives may vary with the sector.

But with all the sectors is a need to focus on the customer: Holiday travel is a behaviour of individual consumers, their perception of the reality is important.

Now is the time for real marketing: Consumer behaviour in tourism is less determined by the general framework conditions than at the end of the last century. The tourists have in their decisions many degrees of freedom. Consumer research is a necessary base, not only for projections into the future, but to determine the starting point, to have an orientation to formulate own objectives and plans to reach them. Without the consumer, in tourism as in every service industry, you will go nowhere. That does not go not only for the industry and their marketing activities, but as well for politics/tourism related policies.

What do the new demand factors in tourism mean for the different sectors or functions?

For *destinations* it is of utmost importance to recognize the international competition they are in. Master plans and marketing activities need realistic objectives considering not only what one wants to reach but as well what others do, then the own resources (financial and human – which will be limited e.g. with demographic change), and – of course – the consumers' motivation and the trends in consumer behaviour in tourism.

Giving the situation of the demand and its expected future trends, it's not sufficient to have a good product. It's not sufficient either, that the consumer perceives a product as a good one. The product or the destination has to be in the consumer's *relevant set*, and to be judged a *very good choice* within this set.

The same goes for the *industry*, i.e. tour operators and travel agencies, transport companies etc. Tour operators and travel agencies may e.g. take advantage from the fact of the information overload. They can take the role of a guide in the information jungle and thus offer convenience.

Politics have not only to watch carefully the market conditions and how the consumers behave under these conditions. The time to just formulate and express good objectives like *sustainability, strengthening specific regions, support third world countries, stressing the importance of the environment, supporting the European integration through more international travel,* where everybody agrees. They have to identify the contradictions and inconsistencies arising from the whole set of objectives and to find solutions or priorities.

It does not seem very useful to provide funding and financial support for everybody just because he intends to follow one of these objectives. Another challenge for politics is to keep the *social balance* within the source markets: Some experts claim that the economic development tends to widen the distance between the poor and the rich within European societies. But tourism needs a broad base of more or less middle class people with time and money to travel.

Coming back to the tourism demand we can state that the future in a quantitative perspective seems to be quite stable: There is no boom ahead, but no bust either. Of course, the future is predictable only within close limits, and unexpected events (e.g. crisis, terror attacks, war, epidemic diseases) will always cause confusion. Still it is important (and possible) to prepare oneself for the trends that can be identified with some reliability today. Demand potentials for good products are there, but you will not be able to sell just anything to the skilled consumer.

In this way the future is open: Room to move for everybody who has a sound marketing plan or political perspective, and respects the consumer. There is a strong need for *orientation* and decision for every organization involved in tourism: Where do you want to go from now and here? What is your objective? Different paths of development are possible, so you have to decide which road to take. You may call that a vision. While elaborating your vision, you need to have a strong focus on the customer, on what other market actors are doing, and what resources are at hand. Visions will be and have to be different on different levels (pan European, national, regional, local), and different with different destinations or other segments of the industry, but linked to some extent.

Success shall be based on safeguarding the core values (the distinctive qualities and related experiences) while constantly adapting to new market trends. A deep understanding of the consumer and his perpetual learning processes as well as the changing structure of tourism demand is a prerequisite for successful planning. A bright future for both, tourists and the tourism industry is within easy reach. Just take your responsibilities to make it real.

2

Hospitality and Tourism Management Systems

Hospitality and Tourism Management (HTM) is a multidisciplinary field of study with the purpose of preparing people with the expertise, commitment, and skills for management, marketing, and operations positions in the expanding industry that provides food, accommodations, and tourism services to people away from home. As a field of study, Hospitality and Tourism Management is interdisciplinary. It draws upon a wide range of basic disciplines to provide the fundamental knowledge and skills that are required to fulfill the diverse demands placed upon individuals in management positions within the hospitality industry.

Tourism and Hospitality

Tourism and Hospitality in India

As per the Travel and Tourism Competitiveness Report 2009 by the World Economic Forum, India is ranked 11th in the Asia Pacific region and 62nd overall, moving up three places on the list of the world's attractive destinations. It is ranked the 14th best tourist destination for its natural resources and 24th for its cultural resources, with many World Heritage sites, both natural and cultural, rich fauna, and strong creative industries in the country. India also bagged 37th rank for its air transport network. The India travel and tourism industry ranked 5th in the long-term (10-year) growth and is expected to be the second largest employer in the world by 2019.

India has been ranked the "best country brand for value-for-money" in the Country Brand Index (CBI) survey conducted by FutureBrand, a leading global brand consultancy. India also claimed the second place in CBI's "best country brand for history", as well as appears among the top 5 in the best country brand for authenticity and art & culture, and the fourth best new country for business. India made it to the list of "rising stars" or the countries that are likely to become major tourist destinations in the next five years, led by the United Arab Emirates, China, and Vietnam.

Contribution to the Economy

According to the Travel & Tourism Competitiveness Report 2009 brought out by the World Economic Forum, the contribution of travel and tourism to gross domestic product (GDP) is expected to be at US$ 187.3 billion by 2019.

The report also states that real GDP growth for travel and tourism economy is expected to achieve an average of 7.7 per cent per annum over the next 10 years.

Export earnings from international visitors and tourism goods are expected to generate US$ 51.4 billion (nominal terms) by 2019. The travel and tourism sector which accounted for 6.4 per cent of total employment in 2009 is expected to generate 40,037,000 jobs i.e. 7.2 per cent of total employment by 2019.

Foreign Tourist Arrivals

Estimates of foreign tourist arrivals (FTAs) and foreign exchange earnings (FEE) are important indicators of the tourism sector. According to the latest data released by the Ministry of Tourism, FTAs during January 2010 were 491,000 as compared to 422,000 in January 2009, an increase of 16.4 per cent. FEE in US$ terms during January 2010 were US$ 1.21 billion as compared to US$ 941 million in January 2009, a growth of 29.1 per cent.

Moreover, to give a further boost to the tourist arrivals, the Indian Association of Tour Operators (IATO) has drawn up plans to hold roadshows in the US, UK, European Union nations and Australia in 2010 to hard sell India as a tourist hub.

Government Initiative

The campaign 'Visit India Year 2009' was launched at the International Tourism Exchange in Berlin, aimed to project India as an attractive destination for holidaymakers. The government joined hands with leading airlines, hoteliers, holiday resorts and tour operators, and offered them a wide range of incentives and bonuses during the period between April and December, 2009.

Euromonitor International's Travel And Tourism in India report states that the Government of India increased spend on advertising campaigns (including for the campaigns 'Incredible India' and 'Ahithi Devo Bhava'-Visitors are like God) to reinforce the rich variety of tourism in India.

The ministry promoted India as a safe tourist destination and undertook various measures, such as stepping up vigilance in key cities and at historically important tourist sites. It also deployed increased manpower and resources for improving security checks at key airports and railway stations.

Medical Tourism

Despite the economic slowdown, medical tourism in India is the fastest growing segment of tourism industry, according to the market research report "Booming Medical Tourism in India". The report adds that India offers a great potential in the medical tourism industry. Factors such as low cost, scale and range of treatments provided in the country add to its attractiveness as a medical tourism destination.

In addition to the existence of modern medicine, indigenous medical practitioners are providing their services across the country with more than 3,000 hospitals and 726,000 registered practitioners catering to the needs of traditional Indian healthcare. A number of Indian hotels will tie up with professional organisations in a range of wellness fields to enter the wellness services market.

According to a report by RNCOS, medical tourism will grow at a CAGR of over 27 per cent in the period 2009–12 to generate revenues worth US$ 2.4 billion by 2012. The number of medical tourists is anticipated to grow at a CAGR of over 19 per cent to reach 1.1 million by 2012. The report adds that India's share in the global medical tourism industry will climb to around 2.4 per cent by the end of 2012.

Hospitality

The Indian hotel industry is adding over 90,000 more rooms across the country in the next five years to meet the demand. The contribution of the hotel industry to the country's GDP was 6.1 per cent in 2008-09.

- Carlson Group, the global hospitality chain, is bringing its luxury hotel brand Regent to India and has signed an agreement with real estate firm, Pioneer Urban Land and Infrastructure, which will invest US$ 49.97 million for building the first Regent hotel in Gurgaon that will open in 2013.
- The Leela plans to open six more properties by 2013, taking the total number of hotels to 12.
- ITC Ltd expects to add 8-10 hotels in India in the next 3-5 years to the existing 110 that it currently operates.
- The Thailand-based hospitality major, Amari, plans to foray into the Indian market by setting up seven four-star hotels near major airports in the country.

The Road Ahead

According to the latest Tourism Satellite Accounting (TSA) research, released by the World Travel and Tourism Council (WTTC) and its strategic partner Oxford Economics in March 2009:

- The demand for travel and tourism in India is expected to grow by 8.2 per cent between 2010 and 2019 and will place India at the third position in the world.
- India's travel and tourism sector is expected to be the second largest employer in the world, employing 40,037,000 by 2019.
- Capital investment in India's travel and tourism sector is expected to grow at 8.8 per cent between 2010 and 2019.
- The report forecasts India to get capital investment worth US$ 94.5 billion in the travel and tourism sector in 2019.

- India is projected to become the fifth fastest growing business travel destination from 2010-2019 with an estimated real growth rate of 7.6 per cent.
- Preparing for the 2010 Commonwealth Games in Delhi, the Tourism Ministry is exploring the provision of tented accommodation to tourists in Faridabad and Surajkund in nearby Haryana.

According to *World Travel and Tourism Council*, India will be a tourism hotspot from 2009-2018, having the highest 10-year growth potential. The *Travel & Tourism Competitiveness Report 2007* ranked tourism in India 6th in terms of price competitiveness and 39th in terms of safety and security. Despite short-and medium-term setbacks, such as shortage of hotel rooms, tourism revenues are expected to surge by 42% from 2007 to 2017.

Tourism by State

Andhra Pradesh

Andhra Pradesh has a rich cultural heritage and a variety of tourist attractions. The state of Andhra Pradesh comprises scenic hills, forests, beaches and temples. Also known as *The City of Nizams* and *The City of Pearls*, Hyderabad is today one of the most developed cities in the country and a modern hub of information technology, ITES, and biotechnology. Hyderabad is known for its rich history, culture and architecture representing its unique character as a meeting point for North and South India, and also its multilingual culture, both geographically and culturally.

Andhra Pradesh is the home of many religious pilgrim centres. Tirupati, the abode of Lord Venkateswara, is the richest and most visited religious centre (of any faith) in the world. Srisailam, the abode of Sri Mallikarjuna, is one of twelve Jyothirlingalu in India, Amaravati's Siva temple is one of the Pancharamams, and Yadagirigutta, the abode of an avatara of Vishnu, Sri Lakshmi Narasimha.

The Ramappa temple and Thousand Pillars temple in Warangal are famous for some fine temple carvings. The state has numerous Buddhist centres at Amaravati, Nagarjuna Konda, Bhattiprolu,

Ghantasala, Nelakondapalli, Dhulikatta, Bavikonda, Thotlakonda, Shalihundam, Pavuralakonda, Sankaram, Phanigiri and Kolanpaka.

The golden beaches at Visakhapatnam, the one-million-year old limestone caves at Borra, picturesque Araku Valley, hill resorts of Horsley Hills, river Godavari racing through a narrow gorge at Papi Kondalu, waterfalls at Ettipotala, Kuntala and rich biodiversity at Talakona, are some of the natural attractions of the state. Visakhapatnam is home to many tourist attactions such as the INS Karasura Submarine museum (The only one of its kind in India), Yarada Beach, Araku Valley, VUDA Park, Indira Gandhi Zoological Gardens.

The weather in Andhra Pradesh is mostly tropical and the best time to visit is in November through to January. The monsoon season commences in June and ends in September, so travel would not be advisable during this period.

Assam

Assam is the central state in the North-East Region of India and serves as the gateway to the rest of the Seven Sister States. Assam boasts of famous wildlife preserves – the Kaziranga National Park and the Manas National Park, the largest river island Majuli, and tea-estates dating back to time of British Raj.

The weather is mostly sub-tropical. Assam experiences the Indian monsoon and has one of the highest forest densities in India. The winter months (October to April) are the best time to visit.

Assam has a rich cultural heritage going back to the Ahom Kingdom which governed the region for many centuries before the British occupation. Other notable features include the Brahmaputra River, the mystery of the bird suicides in Jatinga, numerous temples including Kamakhya of Tantric sect, ruins of palaces, etc. Guwahati, the capital city of Assam, boasts many bazaars, temples, and wildlife sanctuaries.

Bihar

Bihar is one of the oldest continuously inhabited places in the world with history of 3000 years. The rich culture and heritage of Bihar is evident from the innumerable ancient monuments that are dotted all over this state in eastern India. This is the Place of Aryabhatta, Great Ashoka, Chanakya and many more.

Bihar is one of the most sacred places of various religions such as Hinduism, Buddhism, Jainism, Sikhism & Islam. Famous Attraction includes Mahabodhi Temple, a Buddhist shrine and UNESCO World Heritage Site is also situated in Bihar, Barabar Caves the oldest rockcut caves in India, Khuda Bakhsh Oriental Library the Oldest Library of India.

Delhi

Delhi is the capital city of India. A fine blend of old and new, ancient and modern, Delhi is a melting pot of cultures, religions. Delhi has been the capital of numerous empires that ruled India, making it rich in history.

The rulers left behind their trademark architectural styles. Delhi currently has many renowned historic monuments and landmarks such as the Tughlaqabad fort, Qutub Minar, Purana Quila, Lodhi Gardens, Jama Masjid, Humayun's tomb, Red Fort, and Safdarjung's Tomb. Modern monuments include Jantar Mantar, India Gate, Rashtrapati Bhavan, Laxminarayan Temple, Lotus temple and Akshardham Temple.

New Delhi is famous for its British colonial architecture, wide roads, and tree-lined boulevards. Delhi is home to numerous political landmarks, national museums, Islamic shrines, Hindu temples, green parks, and trendy malls.

Goa

Goa is one of the most famous tourist destinations in India. A former colony of Portugal, Goa is famous for its excellent beaches, Portuguese churches, Hindu temples, and wildlife sanctuaries. The Basilica of Bom Jesus, Mangueshi Temple, Dudhsagar Falls, and Shantadurga are famous attractions in Goa. Recently a Wax Museum (Wax World) has also opened in Old Goa housing a number of wax personalities of Indian history, culture and heritage.

The Goa Carnival is a world famous event, with colorful masks and floats, drums and reverberating music, and dance performances. The celebrations run three days culminating in a carnival parade on fat Tuesday.

Himachal Pradesh

Himachal Pradesh is famous for its Himalayan landscapes and popular hill-stations. Many outdoor activities such as rock climbing, mountain biking, paragliding, ice-skating, and heli-skiing are popular tourist attractions in Himachal Pradesh.

Shimla, the state capital, is very popular among tourists. The Kalka-Shimla Railway is a Mountain railway which is a UNESCO World Heritage Site. Shimla is also a famous skiing attraction in India. Other popular hill stations include Manali and Kasauli.

Dharamshala, home of the Dalai Lama, is known for its Tibetan monasteries and Buddhist temples. Many trekking expeditions also begin here.

Jammu and Kashmir

Jammu and Kashmir is the northernmost state of India. Jammu is noted for its scenic landscape, ancient temples, Hindu shrines, castles, gardens, and forts. The Hindu holy shrines of Amarnath and Vaishno Devi attract tens of thousands of Hindu devotees every year.

Jammu's natural landscape has made it one of the popular destinations for adventure tourism in South Asia. Jammu's historic monuments feature a unique blend of Islamic and Hindu architecture styles.

Tourism forms an integral part of the Kashmiri economy. Often dubbed "Paradise on Earth", Kashmir's mountainous landscape has attracted tourists for centuries. Notable places are Dal Lake, Srinagar Phalagam, Gulmarg, Yeusmarg and Mughal Gardens etc. However, the tourism industry is severely affected by the insurgency.

In recent years, Ladakh has emerged as a major hub for adventure tourism. This part of Greater Himalaya called "moon on earth" comprising of naked peaks and deep gorges was once known for the silk route to High Asia from the subcontinent. Leh is also a growing tourist spot.

Karnataka

Karnataka has been ranked as fourth most popular destination for tourism among states of India. It has the second highest number of protected monuments in India, at 507.

Kannada dynasties like Kadambas, Western Gangas, Chalukyas, Rashtrakutas, Hoysalas and Vijayanagaras, ruled Karnataka particularly North Karnataka. They built great monuments to Buddhism, Jainism, Shaivism.

The monuments are still present at Badami, Aihole, Pattadakal, Hampi, Lakshmeshwar, Sudi, Hooli, Mahadeva Temple (Itagi), Dambal, Lakkundi, Gadag, Hangal, Halasi, Galaganatha, Chaudayyadanapura, Banavasi, Belur, Halebidu, Shravanabelagola, Sannati and many more.

Notable Islamic monuments are present at Bijapur, Bidar, Gulbarga, Raichur and other part of the state. Gol Gumbaz at Bijapur, has the second largest pre-modern dome in the world after the Byzantine Hagia Sophia. Karnataka has two World heritage sites, at Hampi and Pattadakal, both are in North Karnataka.

Karnataka is famous for its waterfalls. Jog falls of Shimoga District is one of the highest waterfalls in Asia. This state has 21 wildlife sanctuaries and five National parks and is home to more than 500 species of birds. Karnataka has many beaches at Karwar, Gokarna, Murdeshwara, Surathkal. Karnataka is a rock climbers paradise. Yana in Uttara Kannada, Fort in Chitradurga, Ramnagara near Bangalore district, Shivagange in Tumkur district and tekal in Kolar district are a rock climbers heaven.

Kerala

Kerala is a state on the tropical Malabar Coast of southwestern India. Nicknamed as one of the *"10 paradises of the world"* by National Geographic, Kerala is famous especially for its ecotourism initiatives. Its unique culture and traditions, coupled with its varied demography, has made it one of the most popular tourist destinations in India. Growing at a rate of 13.31%, the tourism industry significantly contributes to the state's economy.

Kerala is known for its tropical backwaters and pristine beaches such as Kovalam.

Madhya Pradesh

Madhya Pradesh is called the *"Heart of India"* because of its location in the centre of the country. It has been home to the cultural heritage of Hinduism, Islam, Buddhism, Sikhism, Jainism. Innumerable monuments, exquisitely carved temples, stupas, forts and palaces are dotted all over the State.

The temples of Khajuraho are world-famous for their erotic sculptures, and are a UNESCO World Heritage Site. Gwalior is famous for its forts, the Tomb of Rani Lakshmibai, and the Palace of Tansen.

Madhya Pradesh is also known as *Tiger State* because of the tiger population. Famous national parks like Kanha, Bandhavgadh, Shivpuri, Sanjay, Pench are located in MP. Spectacular mountain ranges, meandering rivers and miles and miles of dense forests offering a unique and exciting panorama of wildlife in sylvan surroundings.

Maharashtra

Maharashtra is the second most visited state in India by foreign tourists, with more than 2 million foreign tourists arrivals annually. Maharashtra boasts of a large number of popular and revered religious venues that are heavily frequented by locals as well as out-of-state visitors.

Ajanta Caves, Ellora Caves and Victoria Terminus are the three UNESCO World Heritage sites in Maharashtra and are highly responsible for the development of Tourism in the state.

Mumbai is the most cosmopolitan city in India, and a great place to experience modern India. Mumbai famous for Bollywood, the world's largest film industry. In addition, Mumbai is famous for its clubs, shopping, and upscale gastronomy. The city is known for its architecture, from the ancient Elephanta Caves, to the Islamic Haji Ali Mosque, to the colonial architecture of Bombay High Court and Victoria Terminus.

Maharashtra also has numerous adventure tourism destinations, including paragliding, rock climbing, canoeing, kayaking, snorkelling, and scuba diving. Maharashtra also has several pristine national parks and reserves. The Bibi Ka Maqbara at Aurangabad the Mahalakshmi temple at Kolhapur, the cities of Nashik, Trimbak famous for religious importance and the city of Pune the seat of the Maratha Empire and the fantastic Ganesh Chaturthi celebrations together contribute for the Tourism sector of Mahrashtra.

Orissa

Orissa has been a preferred destination from ancient days for people who have an interest in spirituality, religion, culture, art and natural beauty. Ancient and medieval architecture, pristine sea beaches, the classical and ethnic dance forms and a variety of festivals. Orissa has kept the religion of Buddhism alive. Rock-edicts that have challenged time stand huge and over-powering by the banks of the river Daya. The torch of Buddhism is still ablaze in the sublime triangle at Udayagiri and Khandagiri Caves, on the banks of river Birupa. Precious fragments of a glorious past come alive in the shape of stupas, rock-cut caves, rock-edicts, excavated monasteries, viharas, chaityas and sacred relics in caskets and the Rock-edicts of Ashoka. Orissa is also famous for its well-preserved Hindu Temples, especially the Konark Sun Temple. Orissa is the home for various tribal communities who have contributed uniquely to the multicultural and multilingual character of the state. Their handicrafts, different dance forms, jungle products and their unique life style blended with their healing practices have got world wide attention.

Puducherry

The Union Territory of Puducherry comprises four coastal regions viz-Puducherry, Karaikal, Mahe and Yanam. Puducherry is the Capital of this Union Territory and one of the most popular tourist destinations in South India. Puducherry has been described by National Geographic as "a glowing highlight of subcontinental sojourn". The city has many beautiful colonial buildings, churches, temples, and statues, which, combined with the systematic town planning and the well planned French style avenues, still preserve much of the colonial ambience.

Punjab

Punjab is one of India's most beautiful states. The state of

Punjab is renowned for its cuisine, culture and history. Punjab has a vast public transportation and communication network. Some of the main cities in Punjab are Amritsar, Chandigarh, and Ludhiana. Punjab also has a rich religious history incorporating Sikhism and Hinduism. Tourism in Punjab is principally suited for the tourists interested in culture, ancient civilization, spirituality and epic history. Some of the villages in Punjab are also a must see for the person who wants to see the true Punjab, with their beautiful traditional Indian homes, farms and temples, this is a must see for any visitor that goes to Punjab.

Rajasthan

Rajasthan, literally meaning *"Land of the Kings"*, is one of the most attractive tourist destinations in Northern India. The vast sand dunes of the Thar Desert attract millions of tourists from around the globe every year.

Attractions:

- Jaipur-The capital of Rajasthan, famous for its rich history and royal architecture.
- Jodhpur-Fortress-city at the edge of the Thar Desert, famous for its blue homes and architecture.
- Udaipur-Known as the "Venice" of India.
- Jaisalmer-Famous for its golden fortress.
- Barmer-Barmer and surrounding areas offer perfect picture of typical Rajasthani villages.
- Bikaner-Famous for its medieval history as a trade route outpost.
- Mount Abu-Is the highest peak in the Aravalli Range of Rajasthan.
- Pushkar-It has the first and one of the very Brahma temples in the world.
- Nathdwara-This town near Udaipur hosts the famous temple of Shrinathji.
- Ranthambore-Situated near Sawai Madhopur, this town has one of the largest and most famous national parks in India.

Sikkim

Originally known as Suk-Heem, which in the local language means "peaceful home", Sikkim was an independent kingdom till the year 1974, when it became a part of the Republic of India. The capital of Sikkim is Gangtok, located approximately 185 kilometers from New Jalpaiguri, the nearest railway station to Sikkim. Although, an airport is under construction at Dekiling in East Sikkim, the nearest airport to Sikkim would be Bagdogra. Sikkim is considered as the land of Orchids and mystic cultures and colorful traditions. Sikkim is well known among trekkers and adventure lovers, as West Sikkim has a lot to give them.

Places near Sikkim include Darjeeling also known as the Queen of hills and Kalimpong. Darjeeling, other than its world famous "Darjeeling tea" is also famous for its refined "Prep schools" founded during the British Raj. Kalimpong is also famous for its flora cultivation and is home to many internationally known Nurseries.

Tamil Nadu

Tamil Nadu lies in the southern Indian peninsula, on the shores of the Bay of Bengal. Many great rulers including the Cholas, Pallavas, Pandyas and the Vijayanagara Empire ruled over parts of Tamil Nadu. The state is known for its cultural heritage and temple architecture.

Attractions include Mahabalipuram, famous for its Shore Temple, Kanyakumari, the southernmost tip of India, Auroville, an International Utopian city, Mudumalai Wildlife Sanctuary, Ooty and Kodaikanal, two famous hill stations. The Nilgiri Mountain Railway is a Unesco World Heritage Site

Uttarakhand

Uttaranchal is the 27th state of the Republic of India. It contains glaciers, snow-clad mountains, valley of flowers, skiing slopes and dense forests, and many shrines and places of pilgrimage. *Char-dhams*, the four most sacred and revered Hindu temples: Badrinath, Kedarnath, Gangotri and Yamunotri are nestled in the Himalayas. Haridwar which means *Gateway to God* is the only place on the plains.

It holds the watershed for Gangetic River System spanning 300 km from Satluj in the west to Kali river in the east. Nanda Devi (25640 Ft.) is the second highest peak in India after Kanchenjunga (28160 Ft.). Dunagiri, Neelkanth, Chaukhamba, Panchachuli, Trisul are other peaks above 23000 Ft. It is considered the abode of *Devtas, Yakashyas, Kinners,* Fairies and Sages. It boasts of some old hill-stations developed during British era like Mussoorie, Almora and Nainital.

Uttar Pradesh

Situated in the northern part of India, Uttar Pradesh is important with its wealth of monuments and religious fervour. Geographically, Uttar Pradesh is very diverse, with Himalayan foothills in the extreme north, the Gangetic Plain in the centre, and the Vindhya Mountain Range towards the South.

It is also home of India's most visited site, the Taj Mahal, and Hinduism's holiest city, Varanasi.

The most populous state of the Indian Union also has a rich cultural heritage, and at the heart of North India, Uttar Pradesh has much to offer. Places of interest include Varanasi, Agra, Mathura, Jhansi, Prayag, Sarnath, Ayodhya, Dudhwa National Park and Fatehpur Sikri.

West Bengal

Kolkata, one of the many cities in the state of West Bengal has been nicknamed the City of Palaces. This comes from the numerous palatial mansions built all over the city. Unlike many north Indian cities, whose construction stresses minimalism, the layout of much of the architectural variety in Kolkata owes its origins to European styles and tastes imported by the British and, to a much lesser extent, the Portuguese and French. The buildings were designed and inspired by the tastes of the English gentleman around and the aspiring Bengali Babu (literally, a *nouveau riche* Bengali who aspired to cultivation of English etiquette, manners and custom, as such practices were favourable to monetary gains from the British). Today, many of these structures are in various stages of decay. Some of the major buildings of this period are well maintained and several buildings have been declared as heritage structures. From historical point of view, the story of West Bengal begins from Gour and Pandua situated close to the present district town of Malda. The twin medieval cities had been sacked at least once by changing powers in the 15th century. However, ruins from the period still remain, and several architectural specimens still retain the glory and shin of those times. The Hindu architecture of Bishnupur in terracotta and laterite sandstone are renowned world over. Towards the British colonial period came the architecture of Murshidabad and Coochbehar.

Historic Monuments

The Taj Mahal is one of India's best-known sites and one of the best architectural achievements in India. Located in Agra, it was built between 1631 and 1653 by Emperor Shah Jahan in honour of his wife, Arjumand Banu, more popularly known as Mumtaz Mahal. The Taj Mahal serves as her tomb.

The Golden Temple is one of the most respected temples in India and the most sacred place for Sikhs. The Golden Temple is located in Amritsar, Punjab, India.

The Bahai temple in Delhi, was completed in 1986 and serves as the Mother Temple of the Indian Subcontinent. It has won numerous architectural awards and been featured in hundreds of newspaper and magazine articles.

The Victoria Terminus in Mumbai was built by the British and is a UNESCO World Heritage Site.

The Taj Mahal Palace is an icon of Mumbai.

The Victoria Memorial in Kolkata.

Nature Tourism

India has geographical diversity, which resulted in varieties of nature tourism.

- Water falls in Western Ghats including Jog falls (highest in India).
- Western Ghats
- Kerala backwaters

- Hill Stations
- Wildlife reserves.

Wildlife in India

India is home to several well known large mammals including the Asian Elephant, Bengal Tiger, Asiatic Lion, Leopard and Indian Rhinoceros, often engrained culturally and religiously often being associated with deities. Other well known large Indian mammals include ungulates such as the domestic Asian Water buffalo, wild Asian Water buffalo, Nilgai, Gaur and several species of deer and antelope.

Some members of the dog family such as the Indian Wolf, Bengal Fox, Golden Jackal and the Dhole or Wild Dogs are also widely distributed. It is also home to the Striped Hyaena, Macaques, Langurs and Mongoose species. India also has a large variety of protected wildlife.

The country's protected wilderness consists of 75 National parks of India and 421 Sanctuaries, of which 19 fall under the purview of Project Tiger. Its climatic and geographic diversity makes it the home of over 350 mammals and 1200 bird species, many of which are unique to the subcontinent.

Some well known national wildlife sanctuaries include Bharatpur, Corbett, Kanha, Kaziranga, Periyar, Ranthambore and Sariska. The world's largest mangrove forest Sundarbans is located in southern West Bengal. The *Sundarbans* is UNESCO World Heritage Site.

Hill Stations

Several hill stations served as summer capitals of Indian provinces, princely states, or, in the case of Shimla, of British India itself. Since Indian Independence, the role of these hill stations as summer capitals has largely ended, but many hill stations remain popular summer resorts. Most famous hill stations are:

- Pachmarhi, Madhya Pradesh-It is also known as The Queen of Satpura.
- Araku, Andhra Pradesh
- Gulmarg, Srinagar and Laddakh in Jammu and Kashmir

- Darjeeling in West Bengal
- Munnar in Kerala
- Ooty and Kodaikanal in Tamil Nadu
- Shillong in Meghalaya
- Shimla, Kullu in Himachal Pradesh
- Nainital in Uttarakhand
- Gangtok in Sikkim
- Mussoorie in Uttarakhand.

In addition to the bustling hill stations and summer capitals of yore, there are several serene and peaceful nature retreats and places of interest to visit for a nature lover. These range from the stunning moonscapes of Leh and Ladhak, to small, exclusive nature retreats such as Dunagiri, Binsar, Mukteshwar in the Himalayas, to rolling vistas of Western Ghats to numerous private retreats in the rolling hills of Kerala.

Beaches

Elephants and camels rides are common on Indian beaches. Shown here is Havelock Island, part of the Andaman and Nicobar Islands. India offers a wide range of tropical beaches with silver/golden sand to coral beaches of Lakshadweep. States like Kerala and Goa have exploited the potential of beaches to the fullest. However, there are a lot many unexploited beaches in the states of Andhra Pradesh, Gujarat, Maharastra, Tamil Nadu and Karnataka. These states have very high potential to be develop them as future destinations for prospective tourists. Some of the famous tourist beaches are:

- Beaches of Vizag, Andhra Pradesh
- Beaches of Puri, Orissa
- Beaches of Digha, West Bengal
- Beaches of Goa
- Kovalam Beach, Kerala
- Marina Beach, Chennai
- Beaches of Mahabalipuram

- Beaches in Mumbai
- Beaches of Diu
- Beaches of Midnapore, West Bengal
- Andaman and Nicobar Islands
- Lakshadweep Islands.
- Adventure Tourism
- River rafting and kayaking in Himalayas
- Mountain climbing in Himalayas
- Rock climbing in Madhya Pradesh
- Skiing in Gulmarg or Auli
- Boat racing in Bhopal
- Paragliding in Maharashtra.

The Indian Tourism and Hospitality Industry

Tourism and Hospitality Industry

- Hospitality, as an industry segment in itself, is a US$ 3.5 trillion service sector within the global economy.
- In India, the tourism and hospitality industries are witnessing a period of exponential growth; the world's leading travel and tourism journal, "Conde Nast Traveller", ranked India as the numero uno travel destination in the world for 2007, as against fourth position in 2006.
- The year 2007 also marked the fifth consecutive year during which India has witnessed double-digit growth in foreign tourist arrivals.
- Along with the rise in foreign tourist arrivals, foreign exchange earnings have shown a robust growth of 25.6% during January-October 2007 to touch US$ 6.32 billion as against US$ 5.03 billion during January-October 2006.
- Tourism has now become a significant industry in India, contributing around 5.9 per cent of the Gross Domestic Product (GDP) and providing employment to about 41.8 million people.

- As per the World Travel & Tourism Council, the tourism industry in India is likely to generate US$ 121.4 billion of economic activity by 2015 and Hospitality sector has the potential to earn US$ 24 billion in foreign exchange by 2015.
- Additionally, India is also likely to become a major hub for medical tourism, with revenues from the industry estimated to grow from US$ 333 million in 2007 to US$ 2.2 billion by 2012, says a study by the Confederation of Indian Industry (CII) and McKinsey.
- The booming tourism industry has had a cascading effect on the hospitality sector with an increase in the occupancy ratios and average room rates. While occupancy ratio is around 80-85 per cent – up nearly 10 percent from three years back, the average increase in room rates over the last one year has hovered around 22-25%.
- It is pertinent to mention in this context, that according to recent estimates, there are a total of 110,000 rooms in India, as against a total requirement of approximately 250,000 – demonstrating the untapped potential that continues to exist in this industry.
- With a view to stimulating domestic and international investments in this sector, the government has implemented the following initiatives:
  - i. 100% FDI under the automatic route is now permitted in all construction development projects including construction of hotels and resorts, recreational facilities and city and regional level infrastructure.
  - ii. 100% FDI is now permitted in all airport development projects subject to the condition that FDI for upgradation of existing airports requires FIPB approval beyond 74%.
  - iii. A five year tax holiday has been extended to Companies that set up hotels, resorts and convention centres at specified destinations, subject to compliance with the prescribed conditions.

iv. Plans for substantial upgradation of 28 regional airports in smaller towns and the privatization and expansion of Delhi and Mumbai airports

- The aforementioned initiatives have resulted in increasing FDI inflows being witnessed by this industry. For the period April 2000 to November 2007, a total of US$ 636 million in foreign direct investments was channelised towards development of hotels and tourism.
- The hospitality industry has also been receiving increasing interest from the Private Equity Sector – investments have tripled from US$ 60 million in 2004-05 to over US$ 180 million in 2006-07.
- It is estimated that the hospitality sector is likely to see a further US$ 11.41 billion in inbound investments over the next two years.
- Several global hospitality majors such as Hilton, Accor, Marriott International, Berggruen Hotels, Cabana Hotels, Premier Travel Inn (PTI) and InterContinental Hotels group have already announced major investment plans in India in recent years.

Food and Tourism

The concept of 'ethnic food tourism" may have relevance in present days due to increase in tourist industry in the Himalayas. Movement and interaction of people, sense of respect to traditional value and culture will serve to intricately link the enjoyment of dinning to locale, making this the standard of food culture of the region. France attracts the greatest number of tourists worldwide as estimated in 1998 reaching 70 million, which even exceeds the existing population of 58 million. The secret to this appeal is nothing but the delicious food and wine of France, served in inexpensive traditional restaurants that offer the delicious agricultural produce of the region which allows one to experience enjoyment and friendship. Finding enjoyment in eating the produce of the region while in that region – herein lies the essence of a food culture that gives confidence in life, pride to the people of the region and ultimately, enjoyment and friendship. Further, it imparts meaning to the act of travel and bestows happiness upon the traveller. The promoters have to focus on the specific food culture of a region in a presentable form where tourists can find local cuisine in menu.

Ethnic food culture harnesses the cultural history of particular community, their indigenous knowledge of food production, vast nutritious qualities, microbial diversity associated with fermented foods as genetic resources, source of income generation related to tourism and enjoyment of dining.

- Food tourism includes all unique and memorable food experiences, not just four star or critically acclaimed restaurants. Price is not necessarily indicative of quality. According to industry research, true food tourists are perfectly happy at a roadside cafe in the middle of nowhere, as long as there is something memorable about their visit.
- Tourist consumers were asked to list aspects that make a place a good food destination.

Activities

In addition to sampling local food and dishes, food tourists are also likely to engage in the following activities during their holiday:

- Visit museums
- Go shopping
- Attend music and/or film festivals
- Participate in general outdoor recreation.

Accommodation Preferences

- In an in-depth survey of 11 consumers regarding their perception of restaurants and destination, 91% of respondents indicated they choose their accommodation based on the availability of restaurants in the area. One consumer revealed this was because it was less restrictive price-wise, (i.e. more choice), while others mentioned the benefits of proximity, and being able to walk to and from restaurants.

- One consumer did not consider the availability of restaurants to be an important factor in their accommodation decision. This was because they simply expected most city-located accommodation to be situated near restaurant facilities.

Travel Party

Of the total domestic visitors who ate out and/or visited restaurants during their overnight trip, 31% were travelling as part of an adult couple and 24% were travelling alone.

Family groups (ie, parents and children) and friends and/or relatives travelling together (without children) each accounted for a further 19%.

Information Sources

Travellers on holiday use the following sources of information when selecting a restaurant:

- Travel guides
- Brochures from travel agencies
- Newspaper articles
- Magazines
- TV programs
- Word of mouth
- The internet
- Consumer's own knowledge
- Menu shopping.

Length of Trip

Domestic visitors who engaged in the activity of eating out and/or dining at restaurants stayed for an average of 4.5 nights on their trip. By comparison, the average length of stay for all domestic visitors was 4.0 nights.

Barriers

- Many who attempt to define food and culinary tourism immediately think of wineries and fine restaurants. These are two components of the niche, but by no means a definitive list. Food tourism can occur at a farmers' market, or even in the home of a friend or relative.

- Travellers do not often choose their holiday destination based on the food tourism experiences they anticipate to encounter, but still end up remembering their holiday to a certain extent on the quality of the food they experienced at the destination. This creates a conundrum in that many tourists choose holiday destinations based on one perceived aspect (e.g. beaches, accommodation etc.), but their actual satisfaction will be based on aspects (ie, food) they did not consider in their original holiday choice.
- According to research conducted into what aspects of food tourism consumers find appealing, 73% said that a variety of eating options was an important consideration in their destination choice. This automatically biases tourist consumers towards more developed destinations that receive a sufficient volume of visitors to support a diverse food industry. Only 36% of respondents mentioned regional food as being important.

Opportunities

- The food tourism niche market presents a new aspect of destination marketing, which can enhance the attractiveness of a destination without necessarily involving extensive new product development. Food tourism can essentially be viewed as a subset of cultural tourism, with the local cuisine being a product of the local culture and the natural environment. Therefore, regions that possess unique dishes and food products as a result of their culture and environment may be transformed into food tourism destinations with minimum marketing and product development.
- In terms of regional aspects, food tourism can be divided into a rural and an urban/city experience. The urban/city experience usually presents travellers with a wide variety of food tourism products, and convenience in the form of restaurant precincts and culturally distinct cuisine. Rural

food tourism on the other hand is not usually considered as a developed tourism product. Activities such as visits to farms and farmers' markets, fruit picking and agricultural farm accommodation may provide important supplemental activities to struggling rural areas.

- Research suggests that in many instances, consumers attribute their lack of satisfaction with food on their holiday to the reason their trip did not become an overall memorable holiday. Destinations could develop higher consumer satisfaction levels (and hence higher return and recommendation rates) if they could guide tourists to food products that provide memorable experiences (whether it is service, quality, value for money, or uniqueness). This may be achieved through either consumer marketing (e.g. a tourist restaurant/food tourism brochure) or through cooperative product development.
- No state or local food tourism associations currently exist in Queensland. The marketing and development of new food tourism products could be assisted and facilitated by the formation of such an organisation. Membership could also act as a strong indicator to consumers of quality tourism food product.

Marketing

- A large proportion of consumers emphasise a variety of food product as being important in their overall satisfaction with a destination. Therefore, promoting the variety of restaurants and food products available in a destination may enhance destination attractiveness.
- True food tourism visitors can be accessed via industry associations such as the International Culinary Tourism Association and consumer publications.
- It could be useful to include information relating to the following features in any materials prepared for marketing the food tourism product:
    - o the location (including proximity to other local attractions),

- o access to the property (roads, signage),
- o attractions on the property (gardens, views),
- o leisure opportunities (games, crafts, recreational pursuits), and
- o local area attractions (tourist drives, museums, events).

Culinary Tourism

Judging by the surge since 2001 in the number of times "culinary tourism" has appeared as a subject matter or in a session title in tourism industry conferences and programs, we can see that Culinary Tourism is valued by tourism industry professionals as one of the most popular niches in the world's tourism industry. This makes sense, given recent consumer focus on healthy and organic eating, culinary/food pedigrees, and the simple fact that all travellers must eat. Not every visitor goes shopping or visits museums, but all travellers eat. For anyone who doubts, look at the increase in cooking shows featured on The Travel Channel [Anthony Bourdain No Reservations] or travel shows featured on The Food Network [Rachel Ray's $40 a Day series], as examples.

Culinary Tourism is not just experiences of the highest caliber-that would be gourmet tourism. This is perhaps best illustrated by the notion that Culinary Tourism is about what is "unique and memorable, not what is necessarily pretentious and exclusive". Similarly, wine tourism, beer tourism and spa tourism are also regarded as subsets of culinary tourism.

Indian Food Tourism

The finest of *India's* cuisines is as rich and diverse as it's civilization. It is an art form that has been passed on through generations purely by word of mouth, from *guru* teacher) to *vidhyarthi* (pupil) or from mother to daughter.

The hospitality of the Indians is legendary. In *Sanskrit* literature the three famous words *'Atithi Devo Bhava'* or 'The guest is truly your god' are a dictum of hospitality in India. Indians believe that they are honoured if they share their mealtimes with guests. Even the poorest look forward to guests and are willing to share this meager food with guest.

Lassi-Punjab

Lassi, by far, is the most easiest Indian dish to prepare and is taken cold. It is a good way to beat the scorching heat and get refreshed.

It can prepared in two ways either sweet or salty.

Biryani-Hyderabad

Hyderabadi Biryani is a famous meat and rice dish of *Hyderabad,* India. It is a traditional celebration meal made using goat meat and rice and is the staple of a die-hard Hyderabadi. The blending of *mughlai* and *Telangana* cuisines in the kitchens of the *Nizam* (ruler of the historic Hyderabad State), resulted in the creation of Hyderabadi Biryani.

Halwa-Tirunelveli

This sweet (pronounced locally as ulva) is made from wheat and sugar. *Halwa* is brown and semi-solid in texture and contains lots of *ghee/Vanaspati* which gives it the oily look. It tastes the best when fresh and hot. Tirunelveli Halwa is said to owe its peculiar taste due to the recipe of this region.

Two of the famous halwa stores are *Irutu Kadai halwa (Dark Store halwa),* situated near the *Nellayappar* temple and Shanthi Sweets. The name *Irutu Kadai* of the former store derives from the fact that the looks of the store had been kept unchanged from the date it was started. Till date, there is no bright electrical lamp or even a board display to show the shop name!

Pani Puri/Golgappa/Golgappe-Indian Street Snack

Panipuri or Gol Gappa or Gup chup is a popular street snack in the Indian sub-continent. It comprises a round, hollow *puri,* fried crisp and filled with a watery mixture of tamarind, chilli and potato. The name *panipuri* literally means "water in fried bread". The snack has three major ingredients-Puris, pani (water) and stuffing.

Pesarattu-Andhra Pradesh

Pesarattu is a thicker verison of *Dosa* made specifically in major towns of Andhra Pradesh.

Idly-Kancheepuram

The *idli* is a savory cake popular throughout South India. The cakes are usually two to three inches in diameter and are made by steaming a batter consisting of fermented black lentils (de-husked) and rice.

Kancheepuram Idli as the name goes is from Kancheepuram, a holy city in Tamil Nadu, India. History goes that Kancheepuram Idly is served as *prasadam* (offering) in *Varadharaja Perumal Temple,* a famous Hindu temple dedicated to Lord Vishnu, located in the Kancheepuram. It is a huge Idli (Steamed Rice Cake) which is added with spices.

Why Food Tourism is Becoming more Important?

Today's tourist is more cultured than visitors of 20 years ago, is well travelled, is searching for new experiences, is concerned about the environment, is interested in taking part in a health/ well-being lifestyle and wants to experience the local culture when he goes on holiday.

Trend analyst, Ian Yeoman writes that food is a significant aspect of the tourist's experience of a destination, driven by the growing trends of authenticity and the need to have a high-quality experience. Food tourism shapes gastro destinations such as France, Italy and California whereas in emerging destinations such as Croatia, Vietnam and Mexico food plays an important part of the overall experience.

What are the Trends Shaping our Interest in Food Tourism?

Trend 1: Disposable Income and Spending Patterns

All across world, growing affluence of the populations has a profound impact on consumer spending. Consumers spend a higher proportion of their income on prepared food, gourmet products, eating out and food items with some form of health or ethical benefits.

The key point is that according to Michael Silverstein writing in his book Trading Up: The New American Luxury the consumer has traded up where the product is aspiration or traded down when the product is only function. This is one reason why producers and retailers have focused on quality through products such as Tesco's finest range or ethical consumption, where the consumer will pay a premium for 'fair trade' product.

Trend 2: Demographics and Household Change

According to research by the Future Foundation families are also becoming increasingly democratic in food choice, as children get older they have more influence in what they eat and where the family eats. Children are also spending increasing amounts of time with their grandparents with over two-thirds of children born between 1978 and 1986 being looked after by their grandparents at least once a month, compared to one quarter of those born in 1937 or earlier.

This increase indicates a demand for venues offering facilities that appeal to differing age groups and generations. By 2015, those aged between 45 and 59 will be part of the most populous age group in the United Kingdom.

Households headed by those aged 50 plus will account for around 50% of all households, and this same age group will account for over 39% of all consumers spending on leisure goods and services. In 2004, the 50–64 age groups spent US $24.80 per household per week on restaurant meals, US $2.40 more than the national average — this will be a key market in the future.

Another consequence of longevity is 'lifestyle fragmentation', the idea that life is increasingly being experienced as a series of non-linear events with no set pattern. As characteristics of different age groups becomes blurred and diverse, more people will expect the places they visit to be adaptable to different aspects of their daily lives.

In other words, eating out opportunities suitable for whatever the situations requires — whether this is work, with children or simply eating alone. And finally, rising divorce rates are also good for food tourism, as Michael Silverstein observe that divorcees have to search for new partners and subsequently will take prospective partners out for dinner and away for romantic weekends.

Trend 3: Individualism

Individualism means uniqueness as tourists search out local, fresh and good quality cuisine that reflects the authenticity of the destination. The end of mass customisation has seen Starbucks fail in Australia as the brand is perceived as bland and lacking individuality. Gone are the days of the British tourist wanting 'egg and chips' in Ibiza or American's only eating Kentucky Fried Chicken when in Australia.

Trend 4: The Multi-Cultured Consumer

The whole process of globalization has significantly amplified the meaning of the term multi-culturalism within our social order. Access to an even wider range of ideas and interests has never been easier.

The Internet boom, the expansion in specialist and minority TV channels, the relentless growth in international tourism, etc., combine to stretch perceptions and eliminate that what we might call mono-culturalism; seeing the world through only one set of pre-ordained, inherited notions.

The consumer of today will watch the latest Bollywood film, consume a curry, purchase exotic spices for cooking and will read about Rajasthan in the latest edition of the Lonely Planet. Multiculturalism has now become an everyday concept in the daily life of the consumer; today curry is the United Kingdom's favourite dish.

Trend 5: The Role of the Celebrity Chef and Media

The media has substantial influence in determining food product selection. The influence of celebrity chefs is often referred to as the Delia effect' after the media chef Delia Smith, whose 1998 television programme 'How to Cook' resulted in an extra 1.3 million eggs being sold in Britain each day of the series. The phenomena of Gordon Ramsey with 'Hells Kitchen' and the 'F word' or Jamie Oliver campaign for good wholesome school dinners all drives our interest in good quality real food.

The emergence of the niche food programmes, TV channels and magazines means the food celebrity and expert has been created. Today, that celebrity chef shapes tourism products, whether it is a cookery course with Rick Stein in Padstow or Martin Yan's food cruises across China.

Trend 6: Well-Being and Food

Around 30% of adults say that they have been eating less fat and sugar compared to the previous year and 28% say they are eating less salt, whereas other food groups, notably vegetables, fruit and bread/cereal/pasta/potatoes are on the rise. These trends have transformed themselves into the food industry with Starbucks offering Soya milk, and McDonalds offering salads.

In New York, the city council has banned certain types of fats. The proportion of vegetarians has only increased slightly in the last 20 years, with just over 5% of UK adults reporting themselves to be vegetarian in 2004. However, the number of food venues offering vegetarian options due to its association with healthy eating has increased exponentially along with a perception that vegetarian food in restaurants is more than 'vegetable lasagne' or a 'cheese omelette'.

Restaurants are also aware of specialist diets, whether it is catering for gluten free or the Atkins diet. Consumers will even visit a food nutritionalist or advisor of seek opinion about 'food balance' or 'sensitivity towards certain foods'.

The specialist diet is becoming more mainstream with individuals avoiding certain foodstuffs like 'dairy products' or the promotion of detox diets to cleanse the body. Consumers are therefore becoming ever more demanding and cautious regarding the food they eat.

These concerns and fears can be exploited in order to maximise potential marketing of certain products. However, due to the volatile nature of demands and trends, these requirements are hard to predict. Food providers need to have 'quick response' mechanisms in place to enable them to keep up with dietary fads and health scares.

Trend 7: Food as an Oasis

When on holiday, food becomes the social occasion when busy

people create a 'time oasis', but also to connect with family members and friends who may in general be less time-impoverished. Food becomes a human-space within frequently much harried lives; the notion of the meal as a 'time oasis' seems to be a very powerful theme. As the consumer desire for new experiences increases, the 'authentic' restaurant experience becomes more important. Authenticity is about food that is simple, rooted in the region, natural, ethical, beautiful and human – all of the making for a food tourism destination.

Trend 8: Internet Usage

The world is online whether through your computer or mobile phone. Online restaurant reviews are the norm and companies like www.5pm.co.uk use the easyJet principles of yield management allowing consumer's discounts, reviews, auctions for exclusive restaurants, reservations and for restaurants a distribution system for selling unused capacity.

Trend 9: The Desire for New Experiences and Cultural Capital

Food has an important position and role in the emerging experience economy whether in the preparation of it, knowledge of it or consuming it.

As British sociologist Gershuny notes when discussing the whole concept of cultural capital. We have various skills in different sorts of consumption and organisational participation – we play football, we organise social events for the synagogue or church or mosque, we cook food and give dinner parties, we listen to music.

All of these activities give us different sorts of satisfaction, and different degrees of social status, depending on how fully and effectively we are able to participate in them. So, the growing importance of cultural issues, as a leisure activity and as a point of differentiation, means it is an important trend in food tourism as it is the tourist's knowledge of food that distinguishes them.

This means the food tourist has a desire for new tastes, knowledge and concepts and therefore food creates its own cultural capital – which destinations need to capitalise on. As consumers become richer and more sophisticated, they are drawn to new tastes and more adventurous than previous generations.

Trend 10: The Science of Food

Food tourism is shaped by the geopolitical trends. Today, we have rejected science from the food chain resulting in falling yields per hectare as we have rejected GM foods. Food inflation is rising all over the world, for example milk has doubled in price in the last 12 months Farmers are planting crops for fuel rather than food in the rush for biofuels.

Climate change is more disruptive and unpredictable. Rising temperatures mean less water in parts of the world. Land is becoming more expensive due to the increase in urbanisation, therefore less land for food production.

Because of these reasons, will the world return to science in order to protect future food supplies and increase yields? Does this mean cuisine is going to return to Star trek pills and NASA vac packs? Who knows?

Trend 11: However, the Consumer is a Hypochondriac

Although there is evidence that healthy eating is on the rise, the importance of organic food and a desire to try local produce—the consumer can be viewed as a hypochondriac as what they say and actually do can be two different things.

For example, obesity levels have trebled in the USA since 1980 and the amount of vegetables that people consume has steadily dropped since the 1970s.

On one hand, the French campaign against the company, saying it is a symbol of American imperialism and aggression in the world; promotes an unhealthy lifestyle and there is nothing good about its cuisine, whereas on the other hand, the French love the Big Mac, eating three times as many per head of population compared to Spain, Germany and Italy.

Food Tourism Destinations

Some destinations have begun to realise that there is great potential for food tourism to offer a sustainable tourism product, whether it is the fine wines of California or the great cheeses of France. One of the best examples of food tourism has been the rise in prominence of Ludlow in the United Kingdom as a food tourism destination whether it is festivals, slow food or Michelin star restaurants.

Ludlow from the early beginning of a farmers market has prospered into a major food tourism destination with a density of high quality restaurants, an abundance of local food suppliers in the high street and food festivals and events to attract tourists. Ludlow as a food destination illustrates its success through:

- Using food as a means to create cultural capital and social cachet
- Creating a density of food and drink suppliers which results in a tourism eating and shopping experience
- Creating a local authentic promise based upon good quality and fair pricing
- Creating a unique product better than that found in other regional food destinations
- Producers seeing themselves as being involved in tourism
- Tourism providers focusing on food as a point of difference.

Conclusions

Today, the consumer is better educated, wealthy, has travelled more extensively, lives longer, and is concerned about his health and the environment. As a result food and drink has become more important and have a higher priority amongst certain social groupings.

Too the extent food is the new culture capital of a destination, as if culture has moved out of the museum to become a living experience of consumption. One thing is clear; food must be a quality product, whether it is slow food or fast food. Finally, if food is not for you, there is always the no-food movement which is all the rage in Japan where holiday-makers are flocking to the Arina Hotel in the idyllic Nagano Mountains for a fasting feast!

3

Analysis and Interpretation of Financial Statements

Accounting department-As any industry, the hotel industry deals with personnel, materials, sales, equipment, maintenance etc. There is constant turnover of money. This work of managing money matters is done by the accounting department. The Chief Accountant, a chartered accountant, has a team of accountants, auditors, cashiers and accounting clerks working in the department. Chief Accountant works directly under the executive Assistant Manager. Accounting serves a purpose beyond presenting the historical financial position of a hotel. Timely accounting information, properly presented, is information that management can use to improve future performance and compare income and expenses to past performance and future goals.

The Uniform System of Accounts, endorsed by the American Hotel and Lodging Association, is used to present financial information. Additionally, statistics that are useful in analyzing the financial statements are included. Full supplementary schedules and any backup documentation is available to the owner at any time. We will assist client asset managers in the preparation of their internal reports.

Accounting data is processed using an offsite Application Service Provide (ASP) over the internet. This enables our hotels to input daily revenue and statistical data while accounts payable is processed regularly. The end result is that managers, owners and corporate staff can review financial data on line at any time over the internet using a web browser. Using our ASP accounting is accomplished using the most advantageous arrangement for the hotel. We can either perform all of the accounting, from disbursements to statement processing, at our corporate office or decentralize any portion of the process to the hotel level. At HVS Hotel Management, tight internal and cash controls, combined with strong manager responsibility, are key to maximizing profitability.

Generally Accepted Accounting Principles

Generally Accepted Accounting Principles (GAAP) is the americanized term used to refer to the standard framework of guidelines for financial accounting used in any given jurisdiction which are generally known as Accounting Standards. GAAP includes the standards, conventions, and rules accountants follow in recording and summarizing transactions, and in the preparation of financial statements.

Financial accounting is information that must be assembled and reported objectively. Third-parties who must rely on such information have a right to be assured that the data are free from bias and inconsistency, whether deliberate or not. For this reason, financial accounting relies on certain standards or guides that are called "Generally Accepted Accounting Principles" (GAAP). Principles derive from tradition, such as the concept of matching. In any report of financial statements (audit, compilation, review, etc.), the preparer/auditor must indicate to the reader whether or not the information contained within the statements complies with GAAP.

- Principle of regularity: Regularity can be defined as conformity to enforced rules and laws.
- Principle of consistency: This principle states that when a business has once fixed a method for the accounting treatment of an item, it will enter all similar items that follow in exactly the same way.
- Principle of sincerity: According to this principle, the accounting unit should reflect in good faith the reality of the company's financial status.

- Principle of the permanence of methods: This principle aims at allowing the coherence and comparison of the financial information published by the company.
- Principle of non-compensation: One should show the full details of the financial information and not seek to compensate a debt with an asset, a revenue with an expense, etc.
- Principle of prudence: This principle aims at showing the reality "as is" : one should not try to make things look prettier than they are. Typically, a revenue should be recorded only when it is *certain* and a provision should be entered for an expense which is *probable.*
- Principle of continuity: When stating financial information, one should assume that the business will not be interrupted. This principle mitigates the principle of prudence: assets do not have to be accounted at their disposable value, but it is accepted that they are at their historical value.
- Principle of periodicity: Each accounting entry should be allocated to a given period, and split accordingly if it covers several periods. If a client pre-pays a subscription (or lease, etc.), the given revenue should be split to the entire time-span and not counted for entirely on the date of the transaction.
- Principle of Full Disclosure/Materiality: All information and values pertaining to the financial position of a business must be disclosed in the records.
- Principle of Utmost Good Faith: All the information regarding to the firm should be disclosed to the insurer before the insurance policy is taken.

Accounting Cycle and Financial Statements

Financial statements are official records that document the financial activities of a business. They provide a view into the financial condition as well as the profitability of the business. Financial statements are prepared as part of the accounting cycle.

There are four basic types of financial statements:

Balance Sheet Financial Statement

The Balance Sheet gives a snapshot overview of a company's financial condition at a given point in time. (This differs from the other financial statements in that it is the only one that reflects a single point in time; the other statements report on activities over a period of time. In fact, with a 'beginning' balance sheet and the other statements, you have enough information to build an 'ending' balance sheet for any period of time.)

Remember, it is called a 'balance' sheet because the amount of assets should equal (or 'balance') the sum of the liabilities and owner's equity.

Income Statement

The Income Statement reports on a business' profit and loss from operations over a given period of time.

It can also be referred to as a Profit and Loss Statement or P&L Statement. Depending on financial requirements, businesses will prepare either a Single-Step Income Statement or a Multi-Step Income Statement.

Statement of Retained Earnings

The Retained Earnings Statement shows the changes in the owner's equity in a business over a given period of time by highlighting the equity positions at the beginning and end of the reporting period.

Statement of Cash Flow

The Cash Flow Statement reports on a business' cash flow from operations, financing, and investment activities over a given period. It shows how money has flowed into and out of the company, and generally demonstrates the short-term viability of the company's cash position.

The statement of cash flow also explains how the cash position can change independently of profit — $1 million in sales on credit can make the income statement profitable, but without the cash the company might be in dire financial straits.

The Accounting Cycle is a series of steps which are repeated every reporting period. The process starts with making accounting entries for each transaction and goes through closing the books. Use this tutorial for an overview of the accounting cycle, covering activities required both during and at the end of the accounting period.

Accounting Cycle-Introduction

The Accounting Cycle is a series of steps which are repeated every reporting period. The process starts with making accounting entries for each transaction and goes through closing the books.

Accounting Cycle-Steps During the Accounting Period

These accounting cycle steps occur during the accounting period, as each transaction occurs:

1. Identify the transaction through an original source document (such as an invoice, receipt, cancelled check, time card, deposit slip, purchase order) which provides:
   - o date
   - o amount
   - o description (account or business purpose)
   - o name and address of other party (if practical)
2. Analyze the transaction – determine which accounts are affected, how (increase or decrease), and how much
3. Make Journal entries – record the transaction in the journal as both a debit and a credit
   - o journals are kept in chronological order
   - o journals may include sales journal, purchases journal, cash receipts journal, cash payments journal, and the general journal
4. Post to ledger – transfer the journal entries to ledger accounts

- o ledger is kept by account
- o ledger accounts may be T-account form or include balances
- o (Learn more about the Chart of Accounts.)

Accounting Cycle: Steps at the End of the Accounting Period

These accounting cycle steps occur at the end of the accounting period:

1. Trial Balance – this is a calculation to verify the sum of the debits equals the sum of the credits. If they don't balance, you have to fix the unbalanced trial balance before you go on to the rest of the accounting cycle. (If they do balance you could still have a problem, but at least it balances!)
2. Adjusting entries – prepare and post accrued and deferred items to journals and ledger T-accounts
3. Adjusted trial balance – make sure the debits still equal the credits after making the period end adjustments
4. Financial Statements – prepare income statement, balance sheet, statement of retained earnings, and statement of cash flows (this can occur at other points in time with appropriate adjustments)
5. Closing entries – prepare and post closing entries to transfer the balances from temporary accounts (such as the revenue and expenses from the income statement to owner's equity on the balance sheet).
6. After-Closing trial balance – final trial balance after the closing entries to make sure debits still equal credits.

Accounting Concept of Income

The concept of 'income' is different to the economists and accountants. Economists concept of income is that of 'real income' meaning thereby the increase-in real terms of the ownership funds between two points of time.

In accounting the term income is known as 'net profit'. It was stated earlier:

Sales-Merchandising cost = Gross profit and Gross profit-Expenses of doing business = Net profit

In other words, Revenue-Expenses = Net profit.

These terms are explained below:

Revenue

It is the monetary value of the products sold or services rendered to the customers during the period. It results from sales services and source like interest, dividend and commission etc. For example, sales affected by the business and charge made for services rendered by the business constitutes revenue. However, all cash receipt may nott be revenue.

Thus, money borrowed leads to cash receipt but it does not constitute revenue. Similarly additional capital brought in increases proprietor's funds but it is not revenue.

Expenses/Cost of (Doing Business)

Expenditure incurred by the business to earn revenue is termed as expense or cost of doing business. Examples of expenses are raw materials consumed, salaries, rent, depreciation, advertisement etc.

Cash v/s Accrual Basis of Accounting

Small business, individual professionals and non-trading concerns usually adopt cash basis of accounting. Under this system, incomes are considered to have been earned only when received ill cash and expenses are considered to have been incurred only actually paid.

Hence, under this system the profit or loss of an accounting period is the difference between incomes received and the expenses paid. Though the cash basis of accounting is simple (no adjustment is required) but il loses its comparability.

Under accrual basis all incomes are credited to the period in which earned irrespective of the fact whether received or not. Similarly, all expenses are debited to the period in which incurred irrespective of the fact whether paid or not. It is a scientific basis of accounting, though a bit difficult.

Matching Concept. Requires that expenses should be matched to the revenues of the appropriate accounting period. So we must determine what are the revenues earned during a particular accounting period and the expenses incurred to earn these revenues. It is the matching concept which justifies accrual basis of accounting.

Accruals and Deferrals

Accounting is expected to measure or ascertain the net income of the business during the accounting period. Normally, it is the calendar year (1st January to 31st December) but in other cases it may be Financial year (Ist April to 31st March) or any other period according to the convention of the business community of the area. The combined impact of matching concept and the accounting period concept on accounting has resulted in accruals and deferrals.

Accrued or Outstanding Expenses

It is the term which denotes that expenditure has been incurred during the accounting period but the same has not been paid in cash e.g. Salary, Rent, Wage etc. becoming due but not paid.

Deferred or Pre-paid Expenses

It is the term which denotes that payment in cash has been made "in advance but the full benefit of this payment has not been reaped by the current accounting period, e.g., Insurance paid in advance.

Accrued or Outstanding Income

It is the term which denotes that the income has been earned but the cash has not been received against the same. Income has accrued due but not received e.g. Interest on investments etc.

Differed or Received in-advance Income

It is the term which denotes income which has been received (in cash) in advance but it has not been earned so far e.g. rent received in advance. All the accruals and deferrals arc not be adjusted at the end of the accounting period (end-period adjustments) in order to find out the income of the business during the period under review. The procedure of ascertaining (i) business income and (ii) financial position is being described, in detail below:

In fact, these arc two most important of many objectives of book-keeping. In order to know the profits earned by him he prepares a trading and loss account and in order to know the financial position of his business on the last day of the financial period he prepares a balance sheet.

Such accounts are called 'Final Accounts'. Preparation of final accounts is the concluding step of accounting cycle. In fact, final accounts include a number of accounts (i) Manufacturing/ Production account, (ii) Trading account, (iii) Profit and loss account and (iv) Balance sheet.

Practically balance sheet is a statement but for accounting purposes here it is treated as a part vital accounts.

The preparation of above all or any of the above accounts depends upon the nature of the business being carried on by the business concerned. In case of a manufacturing business manufacturing account, trading account, profit and loss account and balance sheet form the parts of final accounts whereas in case of trading business all other accounts are prepared with the exception of manufacturing account. Each of these accounts provide a specific vital information to businessman to help to control and organize the business activities in a batter way.

Internal Control for Food and Beverage Sales

As in nearly all hotel departments, F&B outlets of a hotel might operate under the following systems:

Manual Systems

In small organizations where the manager or the owner is available in nearly all hotel operations, manual systems are preferred. For, there is no need for an investment in computers, though a lot of human errors, as far as control is concerned, might be observed. The forms that must be used in a manual system are:

Captain Order

This form is a written format of the guest order. This is an internal control document prepared in three copies by the waiter/ waitress. A copy is sent to kitchen for food production, a copy to service bar for the drinks to be prepared and the last copy to the cashier for opening a guest check.

On the captain order, no monetary information takes place.

Rather, the order of the guest, the table no., the waiter ID, and number of guest(s) are only filled.

Captain orders help as to control the relation between the waiter, kitchen, service bar and cashier.

Guest Check (F&B check, "Adisyon")

By recording F&B item prices on the captain order, the cashier prepares the guest check. Had any cancellations or additions from the initial captain order occurred, the cashier should make the necessary changes.

As far as payment is concerned, the guest might opt for:

a) Charging to his/her room. In this case, the waiter shall insert the room number and take the guest signature on the guest check,

b) Cash, Credit Card, Bank Check or personal check. In this case, the waiter shall get the due amount from the guest; bring the collection to the cashier, who shall prepare the necessary legal document for sales along with the various internal control vouchers needed. In manual systems, cash register machine is used for this purpose. To illustrate, the cashier rings up the sale on the cash register and gives the guest the cash register bill.

At the end of his/her shift, the cashier should take the "Z" report from the cash register, attach it to various guest checks opened, the captain orders, and the total cash received in that very shift. Later, it is the responsibility of the Hotel Manager or Accounting Managers to verify the total shown on the cash register tape against the total cash receipts and the total developed from the serially numbered guest checks. While doing so, the unit prices recorded on the guest checks have to be also verified from the price list.

Semi-Automated Systems

In larger organizations, maintaining internal control by observation and one to one verifications is not applicable. In cases where business owners want to benefit from computerized systems but cannot afford financially to set up a fully automated system, it is better to get use of an individual Posting Machine for the various F&B outlets' operations.

In such systems, there is no need for the verification of unit prices on the guest checks as the computer automatically posts the prices.

The other advantage is, as the guest check printed from the posting machine is facing the legal requirements, there is no need to use cash register machine or to create another legal document. At the end of each shift, the cashier shall count the cash receipts and compare them with the total generated from guest checks. The accounting department does the verification.

In semi-computerized accounting systems there is no interface with the other hotel departmental systems. This is one of the biggest disadvantages of this very system since it involves extra control work for other departments and functions. For example, the Night Auditor must control and post all the data again to the Front Office system. This is time consuming and subject to numerous posting errors. In practice, this might generate significant late charge amounts, and hence might affect seriously the financial position of the hotel.

Fully Automated Systems

In big organizations, manual or semi-automated systems cannot be applicable because of the huge amount of the number of transactions, their control, and the large amount of money associated to them.

In fully automated systems, in order to maintain an adequate internal control and information flow, the individual computers must be electronically connected to each other. The major advantages of the system are:

1. On-line information is available
2. No need for re-entering data
3. Minimum internal control requirement.

Debit and Credit

Debit and credit are formal bookkeeping and accounting terms. They are the most fundamental concepts in accounting, representing the two sides of each individual transaction recorded in any accounting system. A debit transaction indicates an asset or an expense transaction, a credit indicates a transaction that will cause a liability or a gain. A debit transaction can also be used to reduce a credit balance or increase a debit balance. A credit transaction can be used to decrease a debit balance or increase a credit balance.

Debits and credits are a system of notation used in bookkeeping to determine how and where to record any financial transaction. In bookkeeping, instead of using addition '+' and subtraction '-' symbols, a transaction uses the symbol DR (Debit) or CR (Credit). In double-entry bookkeeping debit is used for asset and expense transactions and credit is used for liability, gain and equity transactions.

For bank transactions, money in is treated as a debit transaction and money out is treated as a credit transaction. Traditionally, transactions are recorded in two columns of numbers: debits in the left hand column, credits in the right hand column. Keeping the debits and credits in separate columns allows each to be recorded and totalled independently. Where the total of the debit value amounts is lower than the total of the credit value amounts a balancing debit value is posted to that nominal ledger account. That nominal ledger account is now "balanced". An account can have either a credit value balance or a debit value balance but not both.

Origin of the Terms Debit and Credit

The term debit comes from Middle French *debet* from Latin *debitum* "that which is owed" (the neuter past participle of *debere* "to owe"). Debit is abbreviated to Di (for debtor). The term credit comes from the Latin *creditum* meaning "that which is entrusted or loaned" from the past participle of *credere* "to trust or entrust". Credit is abbreviated to Ck (for creditor).

Operational Principles

- Debit generally represents any depletion in the resources held by the entity while credit represents increment of the resources held by the entity. Hence, debits to an account are negative/depletions in the accounting entity's resources while credits are positive/increments in the same.

Real Accounts

- In real accounts any increment in assets held by the entity is reflected by increasing the relevant asset account and depletion by crediting the asset account.
- If any asset account is debited then it is on account of increment in the value or acquisition of that liability or owner's equity which decreases the resources held by the entity.

As the total resources held by the entity cannot indigenously increment themselves the depletion has to be matched with a fall in resources within the entity.

Personal Accounts

- In Personal Accounts debiting the personal account of any external entity increases the value of the liabilities receivable from that entity thus augmenting the resources of the accounting entity.
- Similarly crediting the personal account of any external entity reduces the value of monies receivable from that entity thus reducing the resources of the accounting entity.

Nominal Accounts

- In Nominal Accounts the Expense accounts whenever debited are done as the Expense incurred represents the Goods and/or Services acquired for ssumption by the entity and hence are temporary increments in the resources of the consumers.
- In Nominal Accounts the Income accounts are credited as the Income earned represents the Epistolary representation of an entity

Examples

1. when you pay rent with cash: you increase rent (expense) by debiting, and decrease cash (asset) by credit.

2. when you receive cash for a sale: you increase cash (asset) by debiting, and increase sales (revenue) by credit.
3. when you buy equipment (asset) with cash: You increase equipment (asset) by debiting, and decrease cash (asset) by credit.
4. when you borrow with a cash loan: You increase cash (asset) by debiting, and increase loan (liability) by credit.

Depreciation and Double-entry Book Keeping System

Depreciation

Depreciation is a term used in accounting, economics and finance to spread the cost of an asset over the span of several years.

In common speech, depreciation is the reduction in the value of an asset due to usage, passage of time, wear and tear, technological outdating or obsolescence, depletion, inadequacy, rot, rust, decay or other such factors.

In accounting, however, depreciation is a term used to describe any method of attributing the historical or purchase cost of an asset across its useful life, roughly corresponding to normal wear and tear. It is of most use when dealing with assets of a short, fixed service life, and which is an example of applying the matching principle per generally accepted accounting principles.

Depreciation in accounting is often mistakenly seen as a basis for recognizing impairment of an asset, but unexpected changes in value, where seen as significant enough to account for, are handled through write-downs or similar techniques which adjust the book value of the asset to reflect its current value.

The use of depreciation affects the financial statements and in some countries the taxes of companies and individuals. The recording of depreciation will cause an expense to be recognized, thereby lowering stated profits on the income statement, while the net value of the asset (the portion of the historical cost of the asset that remains to provide future value to the company) will decline on the balance sheet. Depreciation reported for accounting and tax purposes may differ substantially.

Depreciation and its related concept, amortization (generally, the depreciation of intangible assets), are non-cash expenses. Neither depreciation nor amortization will directly affect the cash flow of a company, as both are accounting representations of expenses attributable to a given period. In accounting statements, depreciation may neither figure in the cash flow statement, nor be "added back" to net income (along with other items) to derive the operating cash flow. Depreciation recognized for tax purposes will, however, affect the cash flow of the company, as tax depreciation will reduce taxable profits; there is generally no requirement that treatment of depreciation for tax and accounting purposes be identical. Where depreciation is shown on accounting statements, the figure usually does not match the depreciation for tax purposes.

Because of its non-standardized derivation, depreciation is a key component of EBITDA, a metric used to gauge the worth of a company independent of tax-jurisdiction effects and capitalization structure.

Salvage value is the estimated value of an asset at the end of its useful life. In accounting, the salvage value of an asset is its remaining value after depreciation. This is also known as residual value or scrap value. It is the net cash inflow that occurs when the asset is liquefied at the end of its life. Salvage value can be negative if the residual asset requires special treatment to terminate—for example, used nuclear materials or CRT's containing lead. In economics, depreciation is the decrease in the economic value of the capital stock of a firm, nation or other entity, either through physical depreciation, obsolescence or changes in the demand for the services of the capital in question. If capital stock is C_0 at the beginning of a period, investment is I and depreciation D, the capital stock at the end of the period, C_1, is $C_0 + I\text{-}D$.

Accounting

A company needs to report depreciation accurately in its financial statements in order to achieve two main objectives:

1. matching its expenses with the income generated by means of those expenses, and

2. ensuring that the asset values in the balance sheet are not overstated.

Depreciation is an attempt to write-off the cost of Non Current Asset over its useful life. The word write-off means to turn it into an expense. For example, an entity may depreciate its equipment by 15% per year. This rate should be reasonable in aggregate (such as when a manufacturing company is looking at all of its machinery), and consistently employed. However, there is no expectation that each individual item declines in value by the same amount, primarily because the recognition of depreciation is based upon the allocation of historical costs and not current market prices.

Accounting standards bodies have detailed rules on which methods of depreciation are acceptable, and auditors should express a view if they believe the assumptions underlying the estimates do not give a true and fair view.

Recording Depreciation

For historical cost purposes, assets are recorded on the balance sheet at their original cost; this is called the historical cost. Historical cost minus all depreciation expenses recognized on the asset since purchase is called the book value. Depreciation is not taken out of these assets directly. It is instead recorded in a contra asset account: an asset account with a normal credit balance, typically called "accumulated depreciation". Balancing an asset account with its corresponding accumulated depreciation account will result in the net book value. The net book value will never fall below the salvage value, meaning that once an asset is fully depreciated, no further expenses will be taken during its life. Salvage value is the estimated value of the asset at the end of its useful life. In this way, total depreciation for an asset will never exceed the estimated total cash outlay (depreciable basis) for the asset. The exception to this is in many price-regulated industries (public utilities) where salvage is estimated net of the cost of physically removing the asset from service. (Decommissioning a nuclear power plant is a nontrivial expense.) If the expected cost of removal exceeds the expected raw (or gross) salvage, then the net of the two (called net salvage) may be negative. In this case.

the depreciation recorded on the regulated books may exceed the depreciable basis. Companies have no obligation to dispose of depreciated assets, of course, and many fully depreciated assets continue to generate income.

Recording a depreciation expense will involve a credit to an accumulated depreciation account. The corresponding debit will involve either an expense account or an asset account that represents a future expense, such as work in progress. Depreciation is recorded as an adjusting journal entry.

A write-down is a form of depreciation that involves a partial write off. Part of the value of the asset is removed from the balance sheet. The reason may be that the book value (accounted value) of the fixed asset has diverged from the market value and causes the company a loss. An example of this would be a revaluation of goodwill on an acquisition that went bad.

Methods of Depreciation

There are several methods for calculating depreciation, generally based on either the passage of time or the level of activity (or use) of the asset.

Straight-line Depreciation

Straight-line depreciation is the simplest and most-often-used technique, in which the company estimates the salvage value of the asset at the end of the period during which it will be used to generate revenues (useful life) and will expense a portion of original cost in equal increments over that period. The salvage value is an estimate of the value of the asset at the time it will be sold or disposed of; it may be zero or even negative. Salvage value is also known as scrap value or residual value.

Declining-Balance Method

Depreciation methods that provide for a higher depreciation charge in the first year of an asset's life and gradually decreasing charges in subsequent years are called accelerated depreciation methods. This may be a more realistic reflection of an asset's actual expected benefit from the use of the asset: many assets are most useful when they are new. One popular accelerated method is the declining-balance method. Under this method the Book Value is multiplied by a fixed rate.

*Annual Depreciation = Depreciation Rate * Book Value at Beginning of Year*

The most common rate used is double the straight-line rate. For this reason, this technique is referred to as the double-declining-balance method. To illustrate, suppose a business has an asset with $1,000 Original Cost, $100 Salvage Value, and 5 years useful life. First, calculate straight-line depreciation rate. Since the asset has 5 years useful life, the straight-line depreciation rate equals (100%/5) 20% per year. With double-declining-balance method, as the name suggests, double that rate, or 40% depreciation rate is used.

Activity Depreciation

Activity depreciation methods are not based on time, but on a level of activity. This could be miles driven for a vehicle, or a cycle count for a machine. When the asset is acquired, its life is estimated in terms of this level of activity. Assume the vehicle above is estimated to go 50,000 miles in its lifetime. The per-mile depreciation rate is calculated as: ($17,000 cost-$2,000 salvage)/50,000 miles = $0.30 per mile. Each year, the depreciation expense is then calculated by multiplying the rate by the actual activity level.

Units of Time Depreciation

Units of Time Depreciation is similar to units of production, and is used for depreciation equipment used in mine or natural resource exploration, or cases where the amount the asset is used is not linear year to year.

A simple example can be given for construction companies, where some equipment is used only for some specific purpose. Depending on the number of projects, the equipment will be used and depreciation charged accordingly.

Taxes

When a company spends money for a service or anything else that is short-lived, this expenditure is usually immediately tax deductible in some countries, and the company enjoys an immediate tax benefit. To be eligible for depreciation, an asset must have two features:

1. it has a useful life beyond the taxable year (essentially why it was capitalized in the first place), and
2. it wears out, decays, declines in value due to natural causes, or is subject to exhaustion or obsolescence.

Therefore, when a company buys an asset that will last longer than one year, like a computer, car, or building, the company cannot immediately deduct the cost and enjoy an immediate large tax benefit. Instead, the company must *depreciate* the cost over the useful life of the asset, taking a tax deduction for a part of the cost each year. Eventually the company does get to deduct the full cost of the asset, but this happens over several years. In the US, the IRS's depreciation schedule for any given class of asset is fixed, and is related to typical durability. A computer may depreciate completely over five years; a nonresidential building, usually 39 years. The maximum allowable useful life under US income tax regulations is 40 years. Though the IRS does allow a small choice of permutations for depreciation life and acceleration, it does not allow a taxpayer to invent any arbitrary asset life. Other countries have other systems, many simply eliminate all choice altogether. In these jurisdictions accounting depreciation and tax depreciation are almost always significantly different numbers, as in many instances a form of "accelerated depreciation" can be used for tax purposes to lower (taxable) net income in a given period (or, in some instances, a fixed asset may be allowed to be expensed for tax purposes; Section 179 of the Internal Revenue Code allows for this treatment in some circumstances). Technically, these are not considered "tax reductions" but tax deferrals: lowering taxable income now by increasing expenses should increase future taxable income (and taxes) at a later date.

In the US, there are generally five variables that a taxpayer must take into account when computing the correct depreciation deduction:

1. the depreciation base (the asset's cost basis),
2. the asset's class life (estimated life expectancy of the asset),

3. the applicable recovery period (the number of years the taxpayer can claim depreciation deductions),
4. the applicable depreciation method, and
5. the applicable convention (§ 168(d)(4) of the code—generally the half-year convention).

Economics

In economics, the value of a capital asset is equal to the present value of the flow of services the asset will generate in future, appropriately adjusted for uncertainty. Economic depreciation over a given period is the reduction in the remaining value of future services. Under certain circumstances, such as an unanticipated increase in the price of the services generated by an asset, its value may increase rather than decline. Depreciation is then negative.

National Accounts

In national accounts the decline in the aggregate capital stock arising from the use of fixed assets in production is referred to as consumption of fixed capital (CFC). Hence, CFC is equal to the difference between aggregate gross fixed capital formation (gross investment) and net fixed capital formation (net investment) or between Gross National Product and Net National Product. Unlike depreciation in business accounting, CFC in national accounts is, in principle, not a method of allocating the costs of past expenditures on fixed assets over subsequent accounting periods. Rather, fixed assets at a given moment in time are valued according to the remaining benefits to be derived from their use.

Double-entry Bookkeeping System

The double-entry bookkeeping system was started in 13th century and refers to a set of rules to record financial information in a financial accounting system wherein every transaction or event impacts at least two different accounts. In modern accounting this is done using debits and credits, and serves as a kind of error-detection system: if, at any point, the sum of debits does not equal the corresponding sum of credits, then an error has occurred.

Since there are several different types of errors that can occur which result in equal sums for debits and credits, double-entry accounting is not a guarantee that no errors exist. However, it is still useful.

Significance

Double-entry bookkeeping has been considered a fundamental innovation and a cornerstone of Capitalism by such thinkers as Werner Sombart and Max Weber, Sombart writing in "Medieval and Modern Commercial Enterprise" that: "*The very concept of capital* is derived from this way of looking at things; one can say that *capital, as a category, did not exist before double-entry bookkeeping.* Capital can be defined as that amount of wealth which is used in making profits and which enters into the accounts."

Timeline

Century	*Development Stage*
551-479 BCE	Confucius is described, by Sima Qian and other sources, as having endured a poverty-stricken and humiliating youth and been forced, upon reaching manhood, to undertake such petty jobs as accounting and caring for livestock.
Roman Empire	The origins of a primitive double-entry system may possibly be traced as far back as the Roman Empire, in ""*ex Oratione Ciceronis pro Roscio Comaedo*", and *Naturalis, Historiae Plinii, lib. 2, cap. 7* where the advised system was "*That the one side of their book was used for Debitor, the other for Creditor*" (*Huic Omnia Expensa. Huic Omnia Feruntur accepta et in tota Ratione mortalium sola. Utramque Paginam facit.*).
12th	Later there are traces of the double-entry system in the accounting of the Islamic world from at least the 12th century.
13th	The earliest extant records that follow the modern double-entry form are those of Amatino Manucci, a Florentine merchant at the end of the 13th century.

14th	Some sources suggest that Giovanni di Bicci de' Medici introduced this method for the Medici bank in the 14th century.
15th	By the end of the 15th century, the merchant venturers of Venice used this system widely. Luca Pacioli, a monk and collaborator of Leonardo da Vinci, first codified the system in a mathematics textbook of 1494. Pacioli is often called the "father of accounting" because he was the first to publish a detailed description of the double-entry system, thus enabling others to study and use it.

Accounts

An accounting system records, retains and reproduces financial information relating to financial transaction flows and financial position. Financial Transaction Flows primarily encompass inflows on account of incomes and outflows on account of expenses. Elements of financial position, including property, money received, or money spent, are assigned to one of the primary groups i.e. assets, liabilities, and equity.

Within these primary groups each distinctive asset, liability, income and expense is represented by its respective "account". An account is simply a record of financial inflows and outflows in relation to the respective asset, liability, income or expense. Income and expense accounts are considered temporary accounts, since they only represent the inflows and outflows which are absorbed in the financial position elements on completion of the time period.

Books of Accounts

It does this by ensuring that each individual financial transaction is recorded in at least two different nominal ledger accounts within the financial accounting system. The two entries have equal amounts and opposite signs, so that when all entries in the accounts are summed, the total is exactly the same, in other words the accounts balance. This is a partial check that each and every transaction has been correctly recorded. The transaction is recorded as a "debit entry" (Dr.) in one account, and a "credit"

(Cr.) entry in the other account. A debit entry generally means that value has been added to the account, and a credit entry means that value is being subtracted from the account. The debit entry will be recorded on the debit side (left hand side) of a nominal ledger account and the credit entry will be recorded on the credit side of a nominal ledger account. A nominal ledger has a Debit side and a Credit side. If the total of the entries on the debit side is greater than the total on the credit side of the nominal ledger account then that account is said to have a debit balance.

As there are two entries for each transaction, hence the expression Double-Entry is used. As the total of the debit entries equals the total of the credit entries, when the nominal ledger accounts are listed in columns, the left column for accounts with net Debit balances and the right column for accounts with net Credit balances, then the total of all the Debit balances will equal the total of all the Credit balances. If this does not happen then an error has been made somewhere.

An example of an entry being recorded twice for double-entry bookkeeping would be a supplier's invoice for stationery costing $100. The expense or Debit entry is Stationery Nominal Ledger a/c $100 Dr (showing that $100 has been spent on stationery) and the Credit entry is to the Supplier's Control Nominal Ledger a/c $100 Cr (showing that we now owe the supplier $100). This transaction has now been recorded twice in the financial accounting system and the total value is $100 for both Debit and Credit values.

Double entry is only used within the nominal ledgers. It is not used in the daybooks, which normally do not form part of the nominal ledger system. The information from the daybooks themselves will be taken and used within the nominal ledger and it is the nominal ledgers that will ensure the integrity of the resulting financial information created from the daybooks (provided that the information recorded in the daybooks is correct).

(The reason for this is to limit the number of entries in the nominal ledger: entries in the daybooks can be totalled before they are entered in the nominal ledger. If there are only a relatively small number of transactions it may be simpler instead to treat the daybooks as an integral part of the nominal ledger and thus of the double entry system.) However as can be seen from the examples of daybooks shown below, it is still necessary to check, within each daybook, that the postings from the daybook balance.

The double entry system uses nominal ledger accounts. From these nominal ledger accounts a Trial balance can be created. The trial balance lists all the nominal ledger account balances. The list is split into two columns, with debit balances placed in the left hand column and credit balances placed in the right hand column. Another column will contain the name of the nominal ledger account describing what each value is for. The total of the debit column must equal the total of the credit column.

From the Trial balance the Profit and Loss Statement and the Balance Sheet can then be produced. The Profit and Loss statement will contain nominal ledger accounts that are Income or Expense type nominal ledger accounts. The Balance Sheet will contain nominal ledger accounts that are Asset or Liability accounts.

Bookkeeping process

The book keeping process primarily refers to recording the financial effects of financial transactions only into accounts. The variation between manual and any electronic accounting system simply stems from the latency between the recording of the financial transaction and its getting posted in the relevant account. This delay absent in electronic accounting systems due to instantenous posting into relevant accounts is not replicated in manual systems thus giving rise to primary books of accounts such as Sales Book, Cash Book, Bank Book, Purchase Book for recording the immediate effect of the financial transaction.

In the normal course of business, a document is produced each time a transaction occurs. Sales and purchases usually have invoices or receipts. Deposit slips are produced when lodgements (deposits) are made to a bank account. Cheques are written to pay money out of the account. Bookkeeping involves, first of all, recording the details of all of these source documents into multi-column journals (also known as a books of first entry or daybooks). For example, all credit sales are recorded in the Sales Journal, all Cash Payments are recorded in the Cash Payments Journal. Each column in a journal normally corresponds to an account. In the single entry system, each transaction is recorded only once. Most individuals who balance their cheque-book each month are using such a system, and most personal finance software follows this approach.

After a certain period, typically a month, the columns in each journal are each totaled to give a summary for the period. Using the rules of double entry, these journal summaries are then transferred to their respective accounts in the ledger, or book of accounts. For example the entries in the Sales Journal are taken and a debit entry is made in each customer's account (showing that the customer now owes us money) and a credit entry might be made in the account for "Sale of Class 2 Widgets" (showing that this activity has generated revenue for us). This process of transferring summaries or individual transactions to the ledger is called posting. Once the posting process is complete, accounts kept using the "T" format undergo balancing, which is simply a process to arrive at the balance of the account.

As a partial check that the posting process was done correctly, a working document called an unadjusted trial balance is created. In its simplest form, this is a three column list. The first column contains the names of those accounts in the ledger which have a non-zero balance. If an account has a debit balance, the balance amount is copied into column two (the debit column). If an account has a credit balance, the amount is copied into column three (the credit column). The debit column is then totalled and then the credit column is totalled. The two totals must agree-this agreement is not by chance-because under the double-entry rules, whenever there is a posting, the debits of the posting equal the credits of the posting. If the two totals do not agree, an error has been made either in the journals or during the posting process. The error must be located and rectified and the totals of debit column and credit column recalculated to check for agreement before any further processing can take place.

Once the accounts balance, the accountant makes a number of adjustments and changes the balance amounts of some of the accounts. These adjustments must still obey the double-entry rule.

For example, the "Inventory" account asset account might be changed to bring them into line with the actual numbers counted during a stock take. At the same time, the expense account associated with usage of inventory is adjusted by an equal and opposite amount. Other adjustments such as posting depreciation and prepayments are also done at this time. This results in a listing called the adjusted trial balance. It is the accounts in this list and their corresponding debit or credit balances that are used to prepare the financial statements.Finally financial statements are drawn from the trial balance, which may include:

- the income statement, also known as the statement of financial results, profit and loss account, or P&L
- the balance sheet, also known as the statement of financial position
- the cash flow statement
- the statement of retained earnings, also known as the statement of total recognised gains and losses or statement of changes in equity.

Abbreviations used in Bookkeeping

- A/C-Account
- A/R-Accounts Receivable
- A/P-Accounts Payable
- B/S-Balance Sheet
- c/d-Carried down
- b/d-Brought down
- c/f-Carried forward
- b/f-Brought forward
- Dr-Debit
- Cr-Credit
- G/L-General Ledger; (or N/L-Nominal Ledger)
- P&L-Profit & Loss; (or I/S-Income Statement)
- PP&E-Property, Plant and Equipment
- TB-Trial Balance

- VAT-Value Added Tax
- CST-Central Sale Tax
- TDS-Tax Deducted at Source
- MAT-Minimum Alternate Tax
- EBIDTA-Earnings before Interest, Depreciation, Taxes and Amortisation.
- EBDTA-Earnings before Depreciation, Taxes and Amortisation.
- EBT-Earnings before Taxes.
- EAT-Earnings after Tax.
- PAT-Profit after tax
- PBT-Profit before tax
- Dep-Depreciation.

Debits and Credits

Double-entry bookkeeping is governed by the accounting equation. If revenue equals expenses, the following (basic) equation must be true: assets = liabilities + equity.

For the accounts to remain in balance, a change in one account must be matched with a change in another account. These changes are made by debits and credits to the accounts. Note that the usage of these terms in accounting is not identical to their everyday usage. Whether one uses a debit or credit to increase or decrease an account depends on the normal balance of the account. Assets, Expenses, and Drawings accounts have a normal balance of *debit*. Liability, Revenue, and Capital accounts have a normal balance of *credit*.

On a general ledger, debits are recorded on the left side and credits on the right side for each account. Since the accounts must always balance, for each transaction there will be a debit made to one or several accounts and a credit made to one or several accounts. The sum of all debits made in any transaction must equal the sum of all credits made. After a series of transactions, therefore, the sum of all the accounts with a debit balance will equal the sum of all the accounts with a credit balance.

Debits and credits are then defined as follows:

- debit: A debit is recorded on the left hand side of a T account
- credit: A credit balance is recorded on the right hand side of a 'T' account
- Debit accounts = Asset and Expenses (also debit money received into bank accounts)
- Credit accounts = Gains (income) and Liabilities (also credit money paid out of bank accounts).

4

Restaurant Planning and Management

Planning a restaurant depends on your target market, the type of food you are serving and customer turnover.

Reception

The best place for the reception, where you would take bookings, greet customers and process bills is at the front of the restaurant, near the door.

Bar

It is advisable to have a separate bar near the entrance for diners to wait for companions or for a table to become available.

Circulation

Think about how you want customers to get to their table and how you want meals to be served. This can be forced by the use of furnishings to block throughways etc.

Space

The amount of space you should allow per customer will depend on the type of standard expected by the restaurant. The more upmarket and expensive the restaurant the greater amount of space you should allow. A seated diner will take up to 2ft. (61cm) of floor space from the table therefore 6 sq. ft. should be allows per table for four. To create a busy, buzzy atmosphere you may want to put the tables closer together, however this must be thought through as it may discomfort the diner. This might work in your favour by encouraging faster turnaround times.

Kitchen

A kitchen can either be hidden away or made the focal point of the restaurant (Fifteen, 140 Park Lane). In this case be aware that cooking smells and noise will be present in the restaurant which might upset a few people.

Internal Fittings

The selection of internal fittings will depend on the style of restaurant you are planning. Make sure it is pleasing to the eye and a specialist restaurant designer may be the best choice to aid you. Also the lighting of the restaurant is exceptionally important, it can help enhance the overall mood of the restaurant and the appearance of the food being served.

Menu Driven Business Planning

So you want to open a restaurant? Many people come to me with their plans, and ideas after they have decided to build or open a restaurant. It is my responsibility to assist them in their planning process and determine how clearly they have thought their concept through. I ask them to show me a menu, and if their initial response is 'I haven't getting that far in my planning process yet,' my response is "You haven't started the planning process yet".

A menu is the foundation of any restaurant; Guests will support or avoid a restaurant for its food. Starting with a preliminary menu is a simple and basic approach to restaurant development. Begin with a menu, and you are light years ahead in the restaurant development process. A menu will tell you and your Guest what you are trying to be as a business, and greatly enhance your chances for success.

I view a menu for content, image and pricing. Content (the actual items on the menu) will dictate service staffing needs, level of culinary experience and type of management required. Who will be doing the cooking, do they have experience in this type of food, and how much are you paying them?

Image is how the Guest will perceive the menu. Menu image helps define the targeted clientele and which other restaurants this operation would be competing with. Are the content and image of the menu appealing to your desired clientele? Pricing helps determine a potential restaurant's competitive placement. Is the pricing for the type of food offered competitive with other's in the market area, and does it permit the ability to manage a profitable food cost?

Pricing sets the Guest's expectations in terms of food and service quality. This perception will, in turn, help define appropriate staffing levels. The budgeting process can now begin. Analysis of menu content, image and pricing will tell prospective restaurant operators whether their concept is appropriate for a certain market area.

With a preliminary menu in hand, a prospective operator can target a location that will be convenient and appropriate for their desired clientele. Once a site or facility is selected, sales volumes can be projected based on number of seats, menu pricing and the competitive business analysis. With projected sales volumes, how much an operator can spend to acquire, remodel or build a facility is determined. Leases and/or purchase agreements can now be negotiated.

With a clear menu, competitive analysis, sales forecast and development budget, financing can realistically be sought. A business plan can be derived which, if taken to potential investors will demonstrate what type of return they can anticipate on their investment.

Any restaurant business plan must begin with a menu. A proposed menu provides the basics for many questions that must be answered during the restaurant development process. It creates an image of the restaurant, identifies targeted clientele, and defines the proposed restaurant's competition. A preliminary menu allows a sound basis for business budgeting, tests potential profitability, and dictates the development dollars required for a facility. Most importantly, beginning the business planning process with a menu maintains the focus of ownership on the importance of food and the impact it has on the success of the restaurant.

Pasta Restaurant Marketing Plan

Executive Summary

Sigmund's Gourmet Pasta will be the leading gourmet pasta restaurant in Eugene, OR with a rapidly developing consumer brand and growing customer base. The signature line of innovative, premium, pasta dishes include pesto with smoked salmon, pancetta and peas linguini in an alfredo sauce, and fresh mussels and clams in a marinara sauce. Sigmund's Gourmet Pasta also serves distinct salads, desserts, and beverages. Sigmund's Gourmet Pasta will reinvent the pasta experience for individuals, families, and take out customers with discretionary income by selling high quality, innovative products at a reasonable price, designing tasteful, convenient locations, and providing industry-benchmark customer service. In order to grow at a rate consistent with our objectives, Sigmund's is offering an additional $500,000 in equity. Existing members will be given the first option to subscribe to the additional equity to allow each of them to maintain their percentage of ownership. The portion not subscribed by existing members will be available for prospective new investors.

Situation Analysis

Sigmund's Gourmet Pasta is close to entering their second year of operation. The restaurant has been well received, and marketing is now critical to its continued success and future profitability. The store offers an extensive offering of gourmet pastas. The basic market need is to offer individuals, families, and take out customers fresh, creative, attractive, pasta dishes, salads and desserts. Sigmund's uses homemade pasta, fresh vegetables, and premium meats and cheeses.

Market Summary

Sigmund's Gourmet Pasta possess good information about the market and knows a great deal about the common attributes of our most prized and loyal customers. Sigmund's Gourmet Pasta will leverage this information to better understand who is served, their specific needs, and how Sigmund's can better communicate with them.

Market Demographics

The profile for Sigmund's Gourmet Pasta's customer consists of the following geographic, demographic, and behaviour factors:

Geographics;

- Our immediate geographic target is the city of Eugene with a population of 130,00.
- A 15 mile geographic area is in need of our services.
- The total targeted population is estimated at 46,000.

Demographics;

- Male and female.
- Ages 25-50, this is the segment that makes up 53% of the Eugene market according to the Eugene Chamber of Commerce.
- Young professionals who work close to the location.
- Yuppies.
- Have attended college and/or graduate school.
- An income over $40,000.
- Eat out several times a week.
- Tend to patronize higher quality restaurants.
- Are cognizant about their health.

Behaviour Factors;

- Enjoy a high quality meal without the mess of making it themselves.
- When ordering, health concerns in regard to foods are taken into account.
- There is value attributed to the appearance or presentation of food.

Market Needs

Sigmund's Gourmet Pasta is providing its customers with a wide selection of high-quality pasta dishes and salads that are unique and pleasing in presentation, offer a wide selection of health conscious choices, and utilizes top-shelf ingredients.

Sigmund's Gourmet Pasta seeks to fulfill the following benefits that are important to their customers.

- Selection. A wide choice of pasta and salad options.
- Accessibility. The patron can gain access to the restaurant with minimal waits and can choose the option of dine in or take out.
- Customer service. The patron will be impressed with the level of attention that they receive.
- Competitive pricing. All products/services will be competitively priced relative to comparable high-end pasta/Italian restaurants.

Market Trends

The market trend for restaurants is headed toward a more sophisticated customer. The restaurant patron today relative to yesterday is more sophisticated in a number of different ways.

- Food quality. The preference for high-quality ingredients is increasing as customers are learning to appreciate the qualitative differences.
- Presentation/appearance. As presentation of an element of the culinary experience becomes more pervasive, patrons are learning to appreciate this aspect of the industry.
- Health consciousness. As Americans in general are more cognizant of their health, evidenced by the increase in individuals exercising and health club memberships, patrons are requesting more healthy alternatives when they eat out. They recognize that an entree can be quite tasty, and reasonably good for you.
- Selection. People are demanding a larger selection of foods, they are no longer accepting a limited menu.

The reason for this trend is that within the last couple of years the restaurant offerings have increased, providing customers with new choices. Restaurant patrons no longer need to accept a limited number of options. With more choices, patrons have become more sophisticated. This trend is intuitive as you can observe a more sophisticated restaurant patron in larger city markets such as

Seattle, Portland or New York where there are more choices available.

Market Growth

In 1999, the global pasta market reached $8 billion dollars. Pasta sales are estimated to grow by at least 10% for the next few years. This growth can be attributed to several different factors. The first factor is an appreciation for health conscious food. While not all pasta is "good for you," particularly the cream based sauces, pasta can be very tasty yet health conscious at the same time. Pasta is seen as a healthy food because of its high percentage of carbohydrates relative to fat. Another variable that is contributing to market growth is an increase in the number of hours our demographic is working. Over the last five years the number of hours spent at work of our archetype customer has significantly increased. As the number of work hours increases, there is a high correlation of people that eat out at restaurants. This is intuitively explained by the fact that with a limited number of hours available each day, people have less time to prepare their meals and eating out is one way to maximize their time.

Swot Analysis

The following SWOT analysis captures the key strengths and weaknesses within the company, and describes the opportunities and threats facing Sigmund's Gourmet Pasta.

Strengths

- Strong relationships with vendors that offer high-quality ingredients and fast/frequent delivery schedules.
- Excellent staff who are highly trained and very customer attentive.
- Great retail space that is bright, hip, clean, and located in an upscale mall, suburban neighborhood, or urban retail district.
- High customer loyalty among repeat customers.
- High-quality food offerings that exceed competitors offerings in quality, presentation, and price.

Weaknesses

- Sigmund's name lacks brand equity.
- A limited marketing budget to develop brand awareness.
- The struggle to continually appear to be cutting edge.

Opportunities

- Growing market with a significant percentage of the target market still not aware that Sigmund's Gourmet Pasta exists.
- Increasing sales opportunities in take out business.
- The ability to spread overhead over multiple revenue centres. Sigmund's will be able to spread the management overhead costs among the multiple stores, decreasing the fixed costs per store.

Threats

- Competition from local restaurants that respond to Sigmund's Gourmet Pasta's superior offerings.
- Gourmet pasta restaurant chains found in other markets coming to Eugene.
- A slump in the economy reducing customer's disposable income spent on eating out.

Competition

National Competition

- Pastabilities: offers consumers their choice of noodles, sauces, and ingredients, allowing the customer to assemble their dish as they wish. Food quality is average.
- PastaFresh: has a limited selection but the dishes are assembled with high-quality ingredients. The price point is high, but the food is quite good.
- Pasta Works: offers pasta that is reasonably fresh, reasonably innovative and at a lower price point. The company was sold a few years ago, and consequently the direction of management has been stagnant lately and has resulted in excessive employee turnover.

- Perfect Pasta: has medium-priced pasta dishes that use average ingredients, no creativity, and less than average store atmosphere. Sigmund's is not sure how this company has been able to grow in size as their whole product is mediocre at best.

Local Competition

- Restaurant A: This is an upscale Italian restaurant that has a limited selection of pasta dishes. Although the selection is limited and pricey, the dishes are quite good.
- Restaurant B: An Italian restaurant with a decent pasta selection, however quality is inconsistent.
- Restaurant C: An upscale restaurant with a large wine selection and good salads. Everything else is mediocre at best and over-priced. Service can often be poor.

Service Offering

Sigmund's has created gourmet pastas and salads that are differentiated and superior to competitors. Customers can taste the quality and freshness of the product in every bite. The following are characteristics of the product:

1. Sigmund's dough for the pasta is made with Italian semolina flour.
2. Cheeses are all imported.
3. Vegetables are organic and fresh with three shipments a week.
4. Meats are all top-shelf varieties, organic when possible.

At Sigmund's, food is not a product, the experience of dining is a service. Sigmund's prides themselves on providing service that is on par with fine dining. This is accomplished through an extensive training program and only hiring experienced employees.

At a Glance – The Protype Sigmund's Store:

- Location: an upscale mall, suburban neighborhood, or urban retail district.
- Design: bright, hip, and clean.

- Size: 1,200-1,700 square feet.
- Employees: six to seven full time.
- Seating: 35-45.
- Types of transactions: 80% dine in, 20% take out.

Keys to Success

Sigmund's site selection criteria are critical to success. Arthur Johnson, former VP Real Estate, Starbucks, helped us identify the following site selection criteria:

- Daytime and evening populations.
- Shopping patterns.
- Car counts.
- Household income levels.

Critical Issues

Sigmund's Gourmet Pasta is still in the speculative stage as a retail restaurant. Its critical issues are:

- Continue to take a modest fiscal approach; expand at a reasonable rate, not for the sake of expansion in itself, but because it is economically wise to. Continue to build brand awareness which will drive customers to existing stores as well as ease the marketing efforts of future stores.

Marketing Strategy

Sigmund's advertising budget is very limited, so the advertising program is simple. Sigmund's will do direct mail, banner ads, and inserts, with inserts in the Register Guard likely to be the most successful of the campaigns.

Lastly, Sigmund's will leverage personal relationships to get an articles of Sigmund's in the Register Guard. Previous friends who have had their restaurant featured in the Register Guard has seen a dramatic increase of sales immediately after the article was published in the RG.

Mission

Sigmund's Gourmet Pasta's mission is to provide the customer the finest pasta meal and dining experience. We exist to attract and maintain customers. When we adhere to this maxim, everything else will fall into place. Our services will exceed the expectations of our customers.

Marketing Objectives

1. Maintain positive, steady, growth each month.
2. Generate at least $40,000 in sales per month.
3. Experience an increase in new customers who are turned into long-term customers.
4. Realize a growth strategy of one store per year.

Financial Objectives

1. A double-digit growth rate for each future year.
2. Reduce the overhead per store through disciplined growth.
3. Continue to decrease the variable costs associated with food production.

Target Marketing

The market can be segmented into three target populations:

- Individuals: people that dine in by themselves.
- Families: a group of people, either friends or a group of nuclear relatives dining together.
- Take out: people that prefer to eat Sigmund's food in their home or at a different location than the actual restaurant.

The Sigmund's customer are hungry individuals between the ages of 25 and 50, making up 53% of Eugene (Eugene Chamber of Commerce). Age is not the most defined demographic of this customer base; all age groups enjoy pasta. The most defined characteristic of the target market is income. Gourmet pasta stores have been very successful in high rent, mixed-use urban areas, such as Northwest 23rd in Portland.

These areas have a large day and night population consisting of business people and families who have household disposable incomes over $40,000.

Combining several key demographic factors, Sigmund's arrives at a profile of the primary customer as follows:

- Sophisticated families who live nearby.
- Young professionals who work close to the location.
- Shoppers who patronize the high rent stores.

Positioning

Sigmund's Gourmet Pasta will position itself as a reasonably priced, upscale, gourmet pasta restaurant. Eugene consumers who appreciate high-quality food will recognize the value and unique offerings of Sigmund's Gourmet Pasta. Patrons will be both single as well as families, ages 25-50.

Sigmund's Gourmet Pasta positioning will leverage their competitive edge:

- Product. The product will have the freshest ingredients including homemade pasta, imported cheeses, organic vegetables, and top-shelf meats. The product will also be developed to enhance presentation, everything will be aesthetically pleasing.
- Service. Customer service will be the priority. All employees will ensure that the customers are having the most pleasant dining experience. All employees will go through an extensive training program and only experienced people will be hired.

By offering a superior product, coupled with superior service, Sigmund's will excel relative to the competition.

Strategy Pyramids

The single objective is to position Sigmund's as the premier gourmet pasta restaurant in the Eugene, OR area, commanding a majority of the market share within five years. The marketing strategy will seek to first create customer awareness regarding their services offered, develop that customer base, and work toward building customer loyalty and referrals.

The message that Sigmund's will seek to communicate is that Sigmund's offers the freshest, most creative, health conscious, reasonably priced, gourmet pasta in Eugene. This message will be communicated through a variety of methods. The first will be direct mail. The direct mail campaign will be a way to communicate directly with the consumer. Sigmund's will also use banner ads and inserts in the Register Guard. This will be particularly effective because the Register Guard is a popular local paper that is consulted when people are looking for things to do in Eugene.

The last method for communicating Sigmund's message is through a grassroots PR campaign. This campaign will leverage personal relationships with people on staff of the Register Guard to get a couple of articles written about Sigmund's. One will be from the business point of view, talking about the opening of the restaurant and the people behind the venture. This is likely to be run in the business section. The second article will be a food review.

In speaking with many different retailers and restauranteurs, significant increases of traffic followed articles in the Register Guard. Because of this level of effectiveness and low/zero cost, Sigmund's will work hard to get press in the Register Guard.

Marketing Mix

Sigmund's marketing mix is comprised of these following approaches to pricing, distribution, advertising and promotion, and customer service.

- Pricing. Sigmund's pricing scheme is that the product cost is 45% of the total retail price.
- Distribution. Sigmund's food will be distributed through a take out model where customers can call in their order and come to the restaurant to pick it up, come into the restaurant, place the take out order and wait for it to be completed, or come in and dine at the restaurant.
- Advertising and Promotion. The most successful advertising will be banner ads and inserts in the Register Guard as well as a PR campaign of informational articles and reviews also within the Register Guard.
- Customer Service. Obsessive customer attention is the mantra. Sigmund's philosophy is that whatever needs to

be done to make the customer happy must occur, even at the expense of short-term profits. In the long term, this investment will pay off with a fiercly loyal customer base who is extremely vocal to their friends with referrals.

Marketing Research

During the initial phases of the marketing plan development, several focus groups were held to gain insight into a variety of patrons of restaurants. These focus groups provided useful insight into the decisions, and decision making processes, of consumers.

An additional source of market research that is dynamic is a feedback mechanism based on a suggestion card system. The suggestion card system has several statements that patrons are asked to rate in terms of a given scale.

There are also several open ended questions that allow the customer to freely offer constructive criticism or praise. Sigmund's will work hard to implement reasonable suggestions in order to improve their service offerings as well as show their commitment to the customer that their suggestions are valued.

The last source of market research is competitive analysis/ appreciation. Sigmund's will continually patronize local restaurants for two reasons.

The first is for competitive analysis, providing Sigmund's with timely information regarding other restaurant's service offering. The second reason is that local business owners, particularly restaurant owners, are often part of an informal fraternal organization where they support each other's business.

Financials, Budgets, and Forecasts

This section will offer a financial overview of Sigmund's Gourmet Pasta as it relates to the marketing activities. Sigmund's will address Break-even Analysis, sales forecasts, expense forecasts, and how those link to the marketing strategy.

Break-even Analysis

The Break-even Analysis indicates that $40,000 will be needed in monthly revenue to reach the break-even point.

Sales Forecast

The first two months will be used to get the restaurant up and running. By month three things will get busier. Sales will gradually increase with profitability being reached by the beginning of year two.

Expense Forecast

Marketing expenses are to be budgeted so that they are ramped up for months two through four and then lower and plateau from month five to month 10. Restaurants typically have increased business in the fall.

This generally occurs because during the summer, when the weather is nice and it does not get dark until late, people tend to eat out less. From months 10-12, the marketing costs will increase again.

Controls

The purpose of Sigmund's Gourmet Pasta's marketing plan is to serve as a guide for the organization.

Implementation Milestones

The following milestones identify the key marketing programs. It is important to accomplish each one on time, and on budget.

Marketing Organization

Kevin Lewis, the owner, is primarily responsible for marketing activities. This is in addition to his other responsibilities, and does depend on some outside resources for graphic design work, and creativity.

Contingency Planning

Difficulties and risks:

- Problems generating visibility.
- Overly aggressive and debilitating actions by competitors.
- An entry into the Eugene market of an already existing, franchised gourmet pasta restaurant.

Worst case risks may include:

- Determining that the business cannot support itself on an ongoing basis.
- Having to liquidate equipment or intellectual property to cover liabilities.

Sample Menus

Lunch

Appetizers and Small Lunches

- Vegetable Dumplings $7 *Six steamed Chinese vegetable dumplings served with two dipping sauces*
- Fresh Squid Salad $9 *Fresh Squid marinated in garlic, lemons, fresh Italian parsley and extra virgin olive oil*
- Gravlax $9 *Served with honey mustard sauce, mixed greens and grilled toastets*
- Herring Plate $11 *Mustard, Garlic, Tomato, Pickled, Dill & Matje Herring served with boiled potato, sour cream, chives and red onion*
- Swedish Shrimp Salad $11 *Served with lettuce, tomato, yellow asparagus, hard boiled egg in a sweet chill dressing*
- Three Crostini's $7 *Brushetta, Olive Tapanade and Mushroom & Goat cheese*
- Baked Potato $7 *Served with Shrimp & Crab Salad or Curry Chicken Salad*
- Chicken Wrap $8 *Grilled Chicken, carrots, scallion and peanut sauce in a tortilla wrap*
- Joe's Sushi Rolls $11 *Today's home made Sushi rolls. Ask your waiter.*
- Asian Noodles $8 *A cup of Asian noodles, served with fresh edamame and spinach in a sweet Thai chili dressing*
- Tuna Nicoise Ficelles $7 Fresh chunks of tuna, egg slices, tomatoes, red leaf lettuce and black olives

Soup

- Split Pea Soup $5
- Cucumber and Avocado Soup $6 With tomato & basil salad
- Fish Soup small $7 large $9 With saffron, salmon, fresh mussels, claims and lobster meat.

Salads

- Small Mixed Green Salad $6 With house dressing
- Spinach, mushrooms, red onion, yellow peppers and smoked bacon $9 Served with a warm mustard-bacon vinaigrette
- Thai Chicken Salad $11 Tomato, green pepper, cucumber, lettuce and white rice in a spicy sweet Thai dressing
- West Coast Salad $12 Shrimp, crab meat, mussels, green peas, yellow asparagus, tomatoes, mushrooms, green leaf and iceberg lettuce
- Flank Steak Salad $11 Thin slices of flank steak marinated in an Asian dressing and served with mesclun salad and fresh mango
- Gravlax Salad $12 Thin slices of gravlax, mesclun salad, cucumber and sweet mustard dressing
- Vegetarian Salad $11 Spinach, mushrooms, roasted peppers, carrots, eggplant, squash topped with olives and served warm with a lemon-tomato vinaigrette.

Today's Lunch Special $13 Including a Small Salad and Fresh Baked Bread

- Meat: Red Curry Chicken With Basmati rice and fresh steamed broccoli or
- Fish: Grilled Honey Mustard Salmon With red roasted potatoes or
- Pasta: Linguine with fresh pesto sauce.

Today's Business Lunch

Appetizer

- Gravlax or
- Prosciutto Salad.

Entree

- Short Ribs of Beef Served with mango chutney and mashed sweet potatoes with a port wine sauce or
- Dill Crusted Cod Served with roasted potatoes, carrots and citrus broth or
- Swedish Meatballs Served with mashed potatoes, lingon berries and pickled cucumbers.

Dessert

- Coconut Rice Pudding With mango sorbet or
- Chocolate Cake With whipped cream and Raspberry sauce.

Other Lunch Specialties

These menu-items will change every week;

- Smoked Salmon Panini $9 With a Swedish Remoulade
- Tuna and Salmon Burger $12 Served on a sourdough roll with Pineapple Chutney
- Seared Halibut with fresh Spring vegetables $15 Served with a Tomato-Cucumber Feta Salad
- Italian Sausage and Wild Mushroom Risotto $13
- Home made Butternut Squash Ravioli's $13 Served in a white wine sauce with fresh spinach
- Pan-Roasted Chicken with Cognac-Peppercorn Sauce $15 Served with fresh broccoli and mashed potatoes
- Spiced Pork Tenderloin with Pineapple-Avocado Salsa $15 Served with black beans and rice
- Asian Vegetables with Tofu and Coconut milk $13 Fresh vegetables with tofu and coconut milk

- Turkey Burger with Chipotle-Chili Tartar Sauce $12 Served on a bun with arugula, red onion and plum tomatoes
- Plate $13 An assortment of Swedish Delicatesis.

Sandwiches

- Shrimp (open face) $7 Swedish Shrimp, tomato, hard boiled egg, cucumber, lemon aioli and topped with fresh dill, served on white bread
- Meatballs (open face) $7 Swedish Meatballs and pickled beat salad, served on pumpernickel bread
- Turkey Wrap $6 Fresh sliced honey turkey, green lettuce, roasted peppers, sprouts and feta cheese wrapped in a tortilla
- Egg Salad & Tuna Salad $6 Two classics!
- Warm Ham and Pineapple $7 Served with cheese, mixed greens and sweet chili dressing
- Tomato and Mozzarella $6 Served in French Baguette.

Hors d'oeuvre Platters A variety of appetizers;

- For two people $10
- For four people $20
- For six people $30
- For eight people $40.

Dinner

Appetizers

- Small Mixed Green Salad $6 Served with house dressing
- Herring Plate $11 Mustard, Garlic, Tomato, Pickled, Dill & Matje Herring served with boiled potato, sour cream, chives and red onion
- Gravlax $9 Served with honey mustard sauce, mixed greens and grilled toastets
- Plate $15 for two people An assortment of Swedish Delicatesis

- Joe's Sushi Rolls $11 Today's home made sushi rolls. Ask your waiter.
- Mushroom Sauta Torte $7 Served warm with goat cheese
- Oysters with spicy jicama salad $11 Six oysters served on the half shell with a lemon sweet vinaigrette
- Brushetta a la Jacob $7 Chopped tomato, garlic ad fresh basil served on crostini
- Fresh Squid Salad $11 Fresh Squid marinated in garlic, lemons, fresh Italian parsley and extra virgin olive oil
- Spicy Fresh Tuna Tartar $9 Fresh Tuna rolled in cucumber and topped with a spicy chili sesame seed dressing
- Chicken Skewers $8 Served with a tropical peanut dipping sauce
- Prosciutto and Avocado Salad $8 Served with Frisee and Arugula Salad in a lemon vinaigrette.

Entrees

Fish

- Fish Soup $9 With saffron, salmon, fresh mussels, claims and lobster meat
- Sea Bass with Cous Cous Risotto $13 Sauteed Sea Bass with cous cous risotto, green peas and fresh corn
- Roasted Cod with Spinach and Mushrooms $14 Served with red roasted potatoes
- Filet of Mackerel $14 Grilled filet of Mackerel, served with a beet and potato roulade
- Grilled Atlantic Salmon $14 Served with sauteed onions, leeks, artichokes and potatoes in a lemon jus
- Shrimp Charmoula $16 Moroccan Shrimp Skewers marinated in an aromatic herb-and-oil mixture before grilling
- Ahi Tuna with white beans and sundried tomato sauce $15 Seared Ahi Tuna with white beans and a fresh sundried tomato sauce

- Mussel, Clams and Shrimp with saffron risotto $17 Fresh mussels, clams and shrimp in a saffron risotto.

Pasta

- Linda's Pad Thai $12 Pad Thai noodles, garlic, bean sprouts, red and yellow peppers, eggs, leeks, peanuts, tofu in a tamarind-fish sauce. Add shrimp: $3 add chicken: $2
- Angel hair pasta with fresh roma tomatoes, garlic and fresh basil $12 Served in a light white wine sauce with crushed red peppers
- Vegetarian Lasagna $12
- Home made Butternut Squash Ravioli's $14 Served in a white wine sauce with fresh spinach and roma tomatoes.

Meat

- Swedish Meatballs $13 With mashed potatoes, lingon berries and pickled cucumbers
- Chicken Thai $13 Sauteed Chicken Breast pieces in a spicy Thai sauce. Served with jasmine rice.
- Mango Chutney Filet Tenderloin $15 Filet Tenderloins with mango chutney and steamed broccoli
- Duck Breast with orange, honey and champagne sauce $16 Seared duck breast with a sweet sizzling champagne sauce. Served with white beans.
- Rosemary and Garlic Lamb Chops $17 Grilled Lamb chops with red roasted potatoes and red wine sauce
- Pepper Steak $18 Beef Tenderloin with black pepper and cognac sauce. Served with fried potatoes.
- Tornadoes with Bearnie Sauce and Red Wine Sauce $19 Two beef tornadoes, bearnie sauce and red wine sauce. Served with a baked potato.
- Barbecue Beef Ribs $15 Served with baked beans and fried potatoes.

Vegetarian

- Asian grilled vegetables with tofu and black bean sauce $13 Fresh Asian vegetables and tofu in a black bean sauce. Add shrimp: $4
- Steamed mixed vegetables with brown rice $11 Steamed and sauteed with brown rice and soy sauce
- Eggplant Manicotti with ricotta, asiago and spinach filling $12 Sauteed eggplant rolled and stuffed with ricotta, asiago and fresh spinach.

Desserts $6

- Swedish Pancakes Served with Vanilla Ice-cream and fresh berries
- Chocolate Pudding With whipped cream
- Blueberry Cobbler Served with vanilla Ice-cream
- Whole grilled Apples with Vanilla Sauce Warm glazed green apples served with a cold vanilla sauce
- Rhubarb Compote Served with Coconut Ice-cream
- Caramel-Walnut Torte
- Linda's three layer Chocolate Cake Served with whipped cream and raspberry sauce
- Coconut Rice Pudding With mango sorbet
- Swedish Frozen Cheese Cake Chilled and served with fresh berries
- Sparkling Lemon Cream with Biscotti and fresh berries A chilled sparkling wine and lemon sorbet drink served with Biscotti and fresh berries
- Fresh Fruit and Berry Salad
- Ice-cream Today's Ice-cream. Ask your waiter.
- Assorted Cookie and Pastry Platters.

Menu Planning

"Planning a menu" can mean several different things, depending on whom you're talking to. Some cooks think of menu planning as something that only occurs on special occasions, while others plan menus for several days or even weeks before shopping for the ingredients. Factors to consider in menu planning can range from whether the meal is nutritionally balanced to how a meal looks and tastes to how easy it is to serve to a crowd.

The first consideration, nutritional content and balance, is not something I'll address here. Later on I'll discuss the logistics of various types of meal service and menus, but for the most part, this class will concentrate on the gustatory elements of menu planning: how to design a meal that tastes good from beginning to end.

For me, menu planning starts with analysing individual recipes or dishes in terms of flavour profiles and textural elements. Trying to combine dishes into a complete menu without understanding what each contributes to the whole is likely to result in a haphazard collection of food, rather than a progression of complementary dishes. And although there are plenty of times when my "menu planning" consists of opening the refrigerator and pulling out whatever lies within, I try not to inflict that process on my dinner guests.

Taste and Texture

Some of the elements of taste to think about are;

1. how strong the flavours are, and how complex;
2. whether one taste dominates or several blend together;
3. and which of the basic tastes (sweet, salty, sour, bitter and umami if you're inclined to treat that as a separate taste) are present.

This last part is crucial, because the basic tastes interact and influence your palate in very definite ways. Overt sweetness tends to dull the palate; acid tends to "wake it up." A little salt can whet the appetite, but too much is deadening. Likewise with bitter tastes — a little bitterness can be a great palate cleanser, but too much can overwhelm it.

Aside from the basic tastes, you should keep in mind that very strong flavours — garlic, some herbs and spices, very ripe cheeses

— can also overwhelm the palate, which can mean that too much of them too early in the menu will lessen your ability to appreciate what comes after.

Textural elements include

1. how rich the dish is;
2. the acid content (which plays a crucial role in the mouthfeel of the dish);
3. whether the dish is crunchy, smooth, chewy or crisp (to name just a few of the possible textures);
4. and a whole host of sensations known as "chemo-sensory irritations" — the burn of chiles, the heat of mustard or horseradish, the bite of mint and the tingle of carbonation (in drinks).

Probably the most important textural element is the balance of fat and acid, not necessarily within each dish, but within a menu. Fats and oils are wonderful ingredients — they carry flavour, provide a nice "mouthfeel" and give one a sense of satiety. But too much of this very good thing can be cloying and seem to coat your mouth most unpleasantly. Too much acid alone is likewise just nasty. But a touch of acid to cut through the fat (or a bit of fat to round out the acid) provides a balance that works. It's one of the reasons that a simple salad with a tangy vinaigrette is so often served (at least in France) between a heavy meat course and a rich cheese course.

Another element to consider when planning a menu is the complexity of each of the dishes. If you have a very complex main dish – either one with several elements or one with multiple layers of flavour, you might want to consider serving simpler starters or side dishes. For example, if I'm making chicken breasts with a reduction of vermouth and orange juice and finished with cherry tomatoes and capers, I probably don't want to serve it with a gratin of potatoes and cheese or a complicated risotto. If I really want to make the risotto or the gratin, I'll be better off going with a simpler roasted chicken.

Something you've probably noticed is that many of the "main" ingredients we work with as cooks are relatively neutral in taste and malleable in terms of possible textural elements. That is, chicken, beef, tofu, pasta or potatoes can be prepared in very different manners, which will give them different flavour profiles and different textures. Crispy fried chicken will thus suggest different accompaniments than will, say, Thai chicken curry or rolled, stuffed chicken breasts.

Once you've analyzed your individual dishes for these components, you can begin to combine them into a menu.

Balance, Continuity and Contrast

From a gustatory standpoint, a well-designed menu does two things:

- It stimulates the palate but doesn't confuse it.
- It provides a sense of continuity but keeps one's interest with contrasting elements.

Continuity is something that often seems to get lost in many American menus. We draw upon so many different ethnic cuisines that it can be difficult to stick to one (witness the disaster called fusion food). Consider the following menu:

First course: Thai-influenced chicken soup, made with coconut milk and garnished with peanuts

Second course: Salad of sliced tomatoes and fresh mozzarella topped with basil.

Third course: Lamb skewers with mint yogurt sauce.

It's not that any of these dishes were bad on their own. But going from Thailand to Italy to the Middle East is a dizzying journey in the space of one dinner. Unless you have a very good reason, stick with one general cuisine type throughout the dinner.

Also for continuity's sake, it's best to stay with what's seasonal. This doesn't mean that I won't use tomatoes in the winter, but it does mean that I try to stick with dishes that "feel like" summer, or winter (or whatever season) or are at least neutral on that front. Following a spiced pumpkin soup with pasta primavera, for example, is disconcerting to the diner. Before I started to pay much attention to this sort of thing, I served the following menu to some friends. I had fallen into a trap: I really, really wanted to try out a new idea for a salad; but at the same time I'd had a request from one of the guests to make one of my "signature" dishes, beef braised with onions and porter; and I tried to do both. So to start, I had an Italian salad with several types of peppers (including some with a little heat), cherry tomatoes, onion, and olives, garnished with basil. I then followed it with the beef, which I served with mashed root vegetables.

Thus, with one menu, I broke both of the continuity rules. The salad was summery and Mediterranean, while the beef dish (Belgian, incidentally) had a much more fall or winter feeling to it, as did the root vegetable mash. No one complained, but it struck me quite forcefully during the dinner that I'd made a big mistake.

It wouldn't have been tough to remedy. I could have kept the salad but switched to a more Mediterranean preparation for the beef – braised in wine with tomatoes and onions, perhaps. Or, as I've since done, I could have begun with a cabbage salad with carrot and apple, dressed with a warm caraway-studded vinaigrette and garnished with toasted pecans and crumpled crisp bacon.

Finally, think about the level of (for lack of a better word) sophistication of the dish. If you start out with foie gras on savory french toast or caviar and creme fraiche on new potatoes, it's probably better to stick with something on that level, rather than following with a country stew. Such a stark change can be an unwelcome break in the continuity of your meal. And it's just as true in reverse – if you start out with a more rustic dish, you don't want to follow it up with a lobster thermidor (if people actually make that anymore). The good news is that it's pretty easy to give minor tweaks to many dishes to move them up and down the sophistication scale.

Okay, so you want some elements of continuity in any menu. But, naturally, a menu that has no contrasting elements will fail just as miserably as one with no continuity. Of course you can provide contrast with flavour combinations. And textural components that involve the way food breaks against the teeth – whether it's crunchy or smooth, crispy or chewy – should provide plenty of contrast. No one wants a meal that's uniformly smooth and creamy, or so unrelentingly crunchy that it seems more like a dental exercise than a dinner.

But I think that the most crucial type of contrast in a menu is the balance between rich, creamy, fatty foods and acidic or bitter components. Let me illustrate the point with this menu:

First course: Cream of portobello mushroom soup garnished with a chevre/creme fraiche mixture

Second: A caesar-type salad (no egg in the dressing, but very thick) with parmesan and croutons

Third: "Pan roasted" chicken breasts with sauteed mixed mushrooms folded into a sherry cream sauce, served with polenta enriched with cheese and butter

Dessert: an apple and cherry galette topped with cinnamon ice cream. The main flaw with this menu is the sheer volume of rich dairy products. Too much, and too much the same: cream, cream and cheese in the first course; cheese in the second; cream and cheese again in the third and ice cream in the dessert. Not only is the menu incredibly filling, there's no break for the palate: it starts out with major rich and creamy elements and every course repeats them. Overall, even though the dishes themselves may taste fine, the menu is just like a hike across a not terribly scenic plateau: no ups and downs and no relief in sight.

Can it be fixed? It can certainly be improved with some modifications. If you really want the soup, fine, but maybe garnish it with herbs to refresh or some crisped prosciutto (which, yes, is rich, but not creamy, and which would at least add some texture). Then go on with a salad dressed with a tangy vinaigrette. Some bitter greens or maybe toasted walnuts would also help to refresh the palate after the soup.

For the next course, well, if you were set on the mushrooms, then roast them and use them as a base for the chicken breasts (I'd ditch the cheese and cream in the polenta too). A pan sauce with a little sweetness and acid could make the dish much more interesting, and if you felt the need for some fat, you could still enrich it with a little butter without repeating the creamy mouthfeel of the soup.

Progression of Dishes

In most cuisine traditions, menus progress from subtler to more intense flavours, from light to heavy mouthfeel, and (often) from cold to hot dishes. The traditional French haute cuisine menu progression from fish to poultry to red meat may be cliche now, but there are valid reasons for it. As I mentioned previously, too many aggressive flavours can overwhelm the palate, lessening the impact of what comes after. Rich, heavy dishes early in the menu can satiate the diner too soon.

Also, think about this: you want your guests to stay interested in your dinner all the way to the end. If you start out with a showstopper, chances are that your next course will disappoint. Which is not to say that your hors d'oeuvre or first course can't be exquisite; it certainly can be.

Dinner Styles

Before planning your menu, you'll need to decide the format of your dinner: buffet, family style, serial courses, or some combination of the three.

A buffet is, from a service standpoint, the easiest of the three to pull off for a large crowd. From a practical point of view, a buffet works well for a group with differing dietary needs. If your guests include some vegetarians, a cardiac patient, and an Atkins practitioner, a buffet with some dishes that each of them can eat could be your answer. The larger the group of guests, the harder it can be to plan a sequential dinner where the guests can all eat each of the courses. The drawback to a buffet is that since your guests will be eating the various dishes all more or less at the same time, the progression of courses is all but non-existent. Thus you're going to want to prepare a menu of dishes that taste good together, or at the very least, don't clash with one another.

A family style dinner shares some of the elements of a buffet dinner in that your guests can take what they want and skip what they don't. They won't necessarily eat everything together, but the sequence of dishes is not guaranteed. A modified family style dinner can start out with a plated first course (soup, for instance, or a composed salad) and continue with the main course served family style. Such a dinner requires a bit more time for service than does a buffet, but not too much. It gives you some control over the sequence of dishes, but not absolute control.

A dinner with serial courses (usually plated) is the most labour intensive, from the standpoint of service. It also allows (or requires, depending on your viewpoint) you to plan the sequence of dishes with a great deal of control. It will put your guests in the position of not being able to skip any of the dishes without being obvious, so it can lead to some awkwardness if they have any dietary restrictions.

It also limits the time you will be able to spend with your guests, unless you have help serving. If you want to serve a serial multi-course dinner, think hard about the amount of last-minute preparation that each dish will require, and plan accordingly. Get as much done in advance as is humanly possible and write out a detailed timetable for the rest. To keep the pacing of your dinner smooth, it's great if at least one of the courses can be prepared entirely in advance.

The Practical Side of Menu Planning

So much for theory. Now, how do you take all that information and actually come up with a menu? You can start from any of several points: a type of cuisine (Italian, Thai, Mexican), a particular ingredient or ingredients, a particular recipe. Unless you're planning a tasting menu, it's probably easiest to begin with the idea for the main course and work from there, but you can begin with any of the courses. Whatever the dish you begin with, think about the season, the ethnicity of the dish, the flavour profile and the textural elements, and then think about what other dishes will complement it. I think the best way to explain this is to give an example, so here are a couple of menus I prepared along with the planning processes by which I arrived at them.

Menu 1 (Plated, Sequential)

First: Sliced jicama, red and green peppers, and blanched carrots tossed with a lime and jalapeno dressing.

Second: Rock shrimp quesadillas with guacamole.

Third: Pan grilled salmon with a cumin-coriander rub, topped with an orange and chipotle salsa. Served with rice.

For this dinner, I started out with two ideas. I wanted a Southwestern/Mexican menu, and there'd been some great salmon in my local market. Salmon, unlike some other fish, can stand up to some strong flavours, so I started thinking about a spice rub and some type of chile peppers. The orange and chipotle salsa, which also contains lime juice, red onion and cilantro, is something I'd made before and I thought it's go well with the fish. Since the dish would be pretty complex, I decided on plain rice to accompany it.

I thought about starting with the quesadillas and then serving the vegetables, but the flavours in the dressing — lime, chiles, garlic — seemed too similar to the flavours in the salsa. And even though salmon is fairly rich, it still would have been an overload of acid. So I began with the vegetables and kept the quesadillas pretty mild, flavour-wise. The richness of the cheese and guacamole provided a nice contrast to the sharp flavours and acid of both the dressing in the preceding course and the salsa in the last course.

Menu 2 (Modified Family Style)

First: Trio of salads: Roasted eggplant and zucchini salad, Moroccan garbanzo bean salad, Tabbouleh.

Second: Lamb curry served over couscous.

For this menu, I began with the dietary concerns of my guests (one trying to watch calories, the other trying to increase his consumption of whole grains and vegetables). For some reason, grains and vegetables suggested Middle Eastern or Mediterranean food to me, and I started playing around with some ideas for salads. I couldn't make up my mind about which of several to serve, so I finally decided to serve them all, as one course. The curry was made with yogurt, so it was relatively low in calories, yet it provided a creamy texture which, together with the richness of the lamb, balanced the acidity of the salads.

As you can see, neither one of these menus was particularly complex. Your menus don't have to be either. Start out small — two or three courses. Plan family style or modified family style dinners if you find that easier. Remember, you don't have to plan eight-or ten-course tasting menus to rival the French Laundry's. But just putting a little thought into the dishes you prepare, their flavourings and accompaniments, and the order in which you serve them can turn a haphazard meal into a well designed dinner.

Wedding Planner

What to Ask Your Caterer?

Most catering agencies have fixed menus to offer. Find out if they fulfil your requirements. You can 'mix & match' dishes to suit your liking. However, it would not be a bad idea to adhere to their format and select your preferred dishes from there. Find out about any extra charges so that you are not caught unawares at the time of payment.

Seek their opinion since they have more experience than you do. It would be a good idea to put things down on paper as you will be able to compare notes of the various caterers you would have met, before making the final selection. Find out if there are any legal obligations that you may be required to fulfil, especially if you are planning to serve alcohol. The caterer might be able to guide you. Make it a point to have only one staff member of the catering agency attend to your enquiries Ask the person if he/she will be there at the function to ensure that all details are being taken care of. If no, then insist on discussing your plans with the person who will be in charge on the day of your function.

Menu Planing

It would help to have somebody who is well versed in the culinary arts to guide you while finalising the menu. It could be somebody in the family. Make it a point to discuss the final menu with the chef. It will make you feel all that more confident and the chef more involved in abiding by your suggestions. Select items from your menu and ask your caterer for a food trial. This is especially so if you intend to serve either special dishes or a very traditional cuisine. Invite your core group to give their opinion of the food and to suggest any modifications. Take this opportunity to inspect the crockery, glassware, waiters and such like.

Winters & Summers

- Chilly winter weddin Gevening bring to mind hot steaming cups of coffee and piping hot soups. Indulge your guests with a rich traditional cuisine. Ask your organiser to light a big cheery bonfire and make sure that there are enough coal braziers to light up the night! Hire a specialist bartender to do dustice to all those lovely bottles of Cointreau, Triple Sec. Creme de Mentheetal.
- A summer wedding? Avoid heavy, rich Indian curries. Opt for a variety of salads and fresh fruit delicacies. Serve light pasta dishes, fresh juices, mocktails, chaat-papri etc. Avoid milk and cream based preparations as they tend to go rancid in the heat have different flavours of ice-cream instead! Go ahead and hire the ice lolly vendor(chuskiwallah) it's a perennial hit with the young and old alike! For the bar, avoid heavy spirits; instead go in for beer, wines, nimbu-pani, spritzers and coolers! A cool refreshing fruit punch will have people raiding your bar counter and yes! do not run out of ice. Make sure that the venue is air-conditioned or has several pedestal fans and desert coolers.

Do your Homework

Tell the caterer that you would like to attend a function organised by him, prior to your own visit the premises on that day to get a first hand idea of the decor, the waiters' attire etc. Observe whether there are enough of them to ensure a smooth service. Note the food display, cleanliness, hygiene, bins for collecting used plates etc. Check whether the food tastes as fresh as it looks. Take this opportunity to watch how well the car parking is being managed? Are there a sufficient number of attendants? Check the bathrooms for cleanliness.

Are they manned? A word of caution, however. Since you are attending somebody else's function to do your survey, you should have your caterer accompany you. You could also try asking a few guests whether they are happy with the catering, are well attended to etc. Some catering agencies also take care of light arrangements and decor. If your agency does not, then you will find yourself handling the tent house-wallah, florists, musicians et al. In such a situation, you should have a joint meeting, wherein you discuss your various areas of responsibility. This way, you will know who's doing what exactly, and leave no scope for grey areas. Your catering agency could also be called in to cater to the large number of outstation relatives and friends who would have arrived some days prior to the function. You may do a package deal with the caterer. Remember, higher volumes ensure better rates.

Order Food in the Right Quantity

This depends on a lot of factors such as: is the day of your function a very busy date? If yes, you can expect a reduction in the number of guests you have to cater to. A lot of people arrive on the occasion, wish the bridal couple, have a drink or two but do not stay for dinner. Usually, catering agencies work on a guaranteed figure. Check with the caterer as to how much of a margin can he cater to should the number of your guests increase, and the amount of time he would take to make fresh preparations should the need arise. It is better to overestimate than underestimate your numbers and save yourself undue embarrassment.

Buffets

There are different types of service but the most popular is the buffet system, being the most convenient. The wide variety of snacks are arranged attractively on platter, appear fresh, and are easily accessible to all. Having a 'live' counter where snacks are prepared in front of the guests, adds a lively charm to the event. Salads, main course and dessert are laid out on the buffet so that everyone can have exactly what they want and in quantities to their liking.

An important aspect to be mentioned here is that most caterers charge clients on the basis of plates consumed, that is, a certain number of plates are laid out on the buffet counter and the host is charged according to the number of plates. A good tip-have somebody from the family stand at the counter where the plates are being handed over to guests. It is a wonderful welcome feeling when a guest is handed his plate with a lovely smile from a member of the family. In fact, certain communities do adhere to a charming time tested tradition wherein members of the host's family serve the guests themselves. An advantage of 'plate control' is that the host does not get billed for what the musical band, florist and tent personnel ate.

Bar Service

If you are serving alcohol, it is always advisable to have somebody from your core group handle the bar, making sure that the guests are never wanting. This way, unauthorised personnel will not gain access to your stock of bottles. Beer is a fovourite with both men and women, so keep plenty of bottles chilled. Mocktails and ladies drinks such a sherry, gin and tonic etc. should also be kept available, besides the mandatory soft drinks. Remember to pile up on an endless supply of ice cubes.

The All-Important Last-Minute Check

For the function to be completely successful, it is absolutely necessary to check that the catering agency has followed your instructions and specifications to the tee.

- First of all, have all the dishes tasted. It is always better that you do not serve a badly made dish at all rather than have people remember your function with words like, "A splendid evening really, but the chillies in the curry made me cry"
- Check the waiters' uniform and gloves for stains.
- Ensure that all photographic equipment is ready and does not intrude into the gathering. You will not want your guests triping over loose wires, tripods etc. or have the cameramen impose over your guests. They should be as unobtrusive as ever.
- Nothing is as disgusting as having last evening's decorations and flowers hanging limply from their holdings. Check that your florist has removed all the old flowers and provided fresh ones.
- The carpet area should have been swept clean. Chairs must be clean and fans in good working order. Loose electric wires are both dangerous and ungainly to the sight.

Be the Perfect Host

A good host will make his guests feel special from the time of their arrival at the entrance of the venue till the time of departure. Have your core group receive the guests, seat them and have the waiter attend to their refreshments. During dinner, while you have personally ensured that your wedding guests are being well served and are not in want of anything. It is sad albeit true that the bridal couple often gets to eat leftovers from the buffet table, or worse, if nobody ask-does not eat at all. Food might be the last thing on their minds but eat they must. Close family members too might be surviving on excitement and happiness alone. A really good way to solve this dilemma is to have a semi formal sit down towards the end of the function, where the bridal couple, the host and the immediate family, sit down and enjoy a nice meal while recuperating from the evening's events. This is a great time to pop that lovely bottle of champagne and unwind. In the mean time, they must be kept supplied with a regular intake of soft drinks and hor d' oevres to keep their energies flowing.

Payment

Do not forget to ask your caterer about the mode of payment. How much advance are you expected to pay? Will you be liable to pay the entire sum on the night of the function itself ? What are the procedures for cancellations ? Bargain all you can! More often than not, you can get away with a lot and save yourself some money.

Tipping

Speak to your caterer about tipping. Make it clear that you will not tolerate the catering staff soliciting you or your guests for 'baksheesh', or helping themselves to the goodies at the table. You will save yourself from such embarrassments if you deal with reputed caterers only.

Feedback From Guests

Seeking a feedback from your guests is the only way of gauging the success of your wedding arrangements. You will emerge all the more wiser too! While most guests will sing praises out of politeness, some may offer valuable insights. Discuss the report you have gathered with your caterer at the time of final payment-in a frank, constructive and objective manner. Question the mishaps, if any, and give praise where due. It will help you build a long-lasting and mutually beneficial relationship with the caterer. As the axiom goes, a man doesn't change his 'naai' and 'halwai'!

Restaurant Table Service

Life in the restaurant industry is extremely fast-paced, and with every new day comes new challenges. Though you may not be able to predict everything that will go wrong on any given day, with Aloha Table Service you can be prepared to face it head on. Aloha Table Service is the key to reliability and performance for your hospitality POS needs.

Unmatched Performance, Functionality and Features :

- Intuitive touch-screen interfaces
- Built-in redundancy
- User-customisable screens and screen flow
- Menu management
- Comprehensive reporting package
- Microsoft Windows-based
- Several graphical user interfaces
- Performance measurements for servers
- Open architecture
- Off-the-shelf, non-proprietary hardware
- Enterprise capabilities
- Extensive kitchen chit printing options
- Simple cheque or item splitting and combining functionality Aloha Table Service.

Intuitive and Easy-to-use

Table Service's intuitive touchscreens put the user in control with the touch of a finger, making operations and customising the system a snap, allowing you to decrease training time and increase employee productivity. With Aloha, it's easier than ever to enter orders, manage guest checks, run Promotions and process payments.

Powerful Management Functionality

Whether you have weekly promotions or daily menu changes, Aloha's built-in Event Scheduler lets you program events that are automatically activated at a specified time. Special messages can be entered to appear on screen, keeping your employees informed.

Aloha's comprehensive reporting package allows you to keep track of real-time sales results and other data. With extensive front-of-house reporting features like real-time sales statistics, product mix reports, employee check-in stats and server sales, you're able to spend more time with the customer and still keep up with the latest profit margins and performance measures.

Virtual Order Processing

With Aloha Table Service, communication flows sooothly and seamlessly from your wait staff to the kitchen staff. Voids, order changes and adds can now be handled effortlessly through the Aloha system eliminating unnecessary trips to and from the kitchen. And with Aloha's menu item availability feature, you're able to count down selected items or specials as they're ordered so servers never order out-of-stock items-which ensures your customers will continue to receive only the best possible service.

The Table Service Advantage

Aloha Table Service offers advanced point-of-sale functionality, intuitive Window-based touch screens, open architecture, built-in redundancy, extensive front-of-house reporting and much more to meet the exact needs of your business. The peerless pas system provides you with the tools to effectively and efficiently manage your operations. No matter how you configure it, the end result is always a smooth-running, seamlessly integrated system.

Benefits

- Order processing ease
- Powerful management functions

- Unparalleled menu management capacity
- Built-in security system
- Modular, flexible design that allows the system to meet current and future needs
- Detailed report and audit tracking
- Automated scheduled menu and promotion events
- Fast and easy to train.

Life in the restaurant industry is extremely fast-paced, and with every new day comes new challenges. Though you may not be able to predict everything that will go wrong on any given day, with Aloha Table Service you can be prepared to face it head on. Aloha Table Service is the key to reliability and performance for your hospitality POS needs.

Unmatched performance, functionality and features :

- Intuitive touch-screen interfaces
- Built-in redundancy
- User-customisable screens and screen flow
- Menu management
- Comprehensive reporting package
- Microsoft Windows-based
- Several graphical user interfaces
- Performance measurements for servers
- Open architecture
- Off-the-shelf, non-proprietary hardware
- Enterprise capabilities
- Extensive kitchen chit printing options
- Simple cheque or item splitting and combining functionality Aloha Table Service.

Table Reservations

Say goodbye to inefficient and messy manual reservation books, grease pens and dirty rags. ReservIT software accepts reservations from any workstation in your restaurant, across multiple restaurants, even through your company's website.

As you book reservations, this Windows based software actively tracks your guests' history and preferences, so your entire staff can make them feel at home and offer truly personalized service. This information can also be mined to support targeted marketing efforts based on customer habits, birthdays, anniversaries, special request and more. With its easy-to-read screen and point-and-click functionality, ReservIT software reduces errors, centralizes reservations for multiple locations, and lets you process more reservations with fewer people staffing the phones. It's just one of many ways In Touch is changing the industry, providing a wide range of products to increase your revenue, enhance the guest experience, and improve your bottom line.

Table Availability Notification

Visual prompts immediately let host staff know when tables become available, even in large restaurants, multi-level facilities, or enclosed rooms. Faster seating reduces congestion, creates more inviting atmosphere, and increases table turn around. Ability to see the status of the restaurant without walking the floor. Automatic server paging speeds up service, prevents walkouts, makes guests happier, and earns more return visits.

Automated Waiting List

Maximize utilization of tables with the systems automatic suggestions. The AccQuote feature provides precise wait times, reducing customer dissatisfaction and walkouts. Simplified process reduces staff frustration and turnover. PC-based system eliminates paper passing and appearance of confusion.

Balanced Server Rotation

Server rotation system tracks the number of times a server is seated last seated. Eliminate double and triple seating of servers. Sense of fairness keeps staff happier and reduces turnover.

Improved Decision Making

Ability to monitor restaurant status at a glance. Aids day-to-day management. Historical data provides performance benchmarks and reveals new opportunities. Many of the worlds best and busiest restaurants have discovered that the old Book, no longer meets their needs. With Reserved for reservations you now have the tools to allow you to control your operations better.

In Touch Table Management

In Touch ReservIT touch screen software takes the guesswork out of table management, preventing walkouts and getting customers seated in record time.

A customized, colour-coded display of your floor plan shows table status at a glance provides accurate wait times dynamically updated throughout the day based on seating trends and table turns prompts your host staff when space becomes available, and automatically rotates servers to fairly distribute the workload. It's also exceptionally easy to use, reducing training costs and preserving best practices in an industry marked by chronically high turnover.

It's just one of many ways In Touch is changing the industry, providing a wide range of products to increase your revenue, enhance the guest experience, and improve your bottom line.

Guest Recognition

Instant view histories, notes, preferences, current reservations. Reduce time spent constantly taking down names and phone numbers. Help new employees to offer personalized service immediately.

Multiple Points/Multiple Locations

Avoid making guests wait while someone looks for the reservation book. Save time and prevent errors. The Quick View feature provides the ability to view table availability for all restaurants in the system. Provide a central number for all locations.

Reservation List Management

Provide guests with options of different reservations at multiple locations. Add guests to a computerized wait list and eliminate mistakes. Enhanced automatic table selection method designed to increase seat usage efficiency when selecting tables for a reservation.

Automatically releases selected tables when the party size is decreased, and selects additional tables when party size is increased.

Customer Relationship Marketing

Base promotions on specific histories, preferences, holidays, special requests, etc. Increase number and frequency of future visits. Save money by focusing your marketing efforts.

The ReservIT floor plan shows the current status of all your guests. Seating allocation is a simple point and click operation and you are able to look at individual sections or the total tables in the outlet. Interfacing to your POS system provides immediate feedback to your hostess.

Restaurant Food Safety-Critical for Success

A little more than a decade after global warming, gradually disappearing rain forests and endangered species ruled our collective conscience, new concerns have started to dominate our concerns: pesticides, mad cow disease, *e-coli* genetically modified foods, fungicides, growth hormones and food safety.

In this first decade of the 21st century, food safety is the environmental issue (75 percent of North Americans claim to be concerned about the wholesomeness of the food they consume). Even a larger percentage is concerned about processed food, yet a huge proportion of the population buys processed and prepared food due to time constraints. These days, people are time poor but cash rich. Considering the fact that in the recent past more ground beef had to be recalled than anytime before 1990 shows how vulnerable we all are.

It used to be that food manufacturers wanting to export to Canada had to pass stringent health inspections carried out by specially trained officials before they were allowed to ship a unit of their product, but this policy has been relaxed. Also every slaughterhouse had to have an inspector (provincial or federal) but this policy has been relaxed in most cases.

These days the North American consumer has more opportunity to sample food from different part of the world. You can now buy haricot beans from Kenya, Kiwi from New Zealand,

Israel, Chile, or Italy, pineapple from Thailand, herbs from Costa Rica, avocados from the Caribbean, avocado oil from New Zealand, papayas from Brazil, okra from India and mangoes from Central, America oysters from France, swordfish from Chile, cod from Norway and even dried fish from Maldives. Some of these foods may be contaminated due to illegal means of irrigation with untreated sewage.

Restaurants are just one link in the food-supply chain; their role against food borne illness is crucial. In Canada approximately 10,000 cases of food borne diseases are reported annually, of which 30 percent result in death. The Atlanta based Centre of Disease Control (CDC) estimates that about 70 percent of all food borne illness outbreaks occur in foodservice operation compared to 20 percent traced to homes. Food processors account for three percent but this figure is increasing.

It is obvious that the restaurant industry particularly the fast food industry must train all food handlers more vigorously, hire healthy individuals and take every possible precaution to serve wholesome foods. This will cost but it better to be safe than sorry. I can recall a few ago the Jack-in-the-Box tragedy that cost millions and even more in lost business and reputation. All equipment and literature are readily available at affordable cost. Managers just need to implement a well thought out education seminar, then maintain standards. Ingesting food that has been contaminated by bacteria, viruses, parasites or chemicals causes food borne illness. Food-safety hazards can be introduced into food service operations in a number of ways, such as food, equipment, supplies and customers. The hazards may be biological (bacteria, viruses, parasites and fungi); chemical (cleaning supplies, pesticides, and food additives); or physical (dirt, broken glass and crockery that accidentally get into food).

Diseases can also be spread by cross-contamination, which is the transfer of harmful substances or microorganisms to food by a variety of means. Utensils, washcloths, and human hands can contaminate ready-to-eat foods. Contamination can also occur via food-to-food, such as when thawing meats drip on ready-to-eat foods.

5

Financial Auditing of Hospitality Industry

Balance Sheet

In financial accounting, a balance sheet or statement of financial position is a summary of the financial balances of a sole proprietorship, a business partnership or a company. Assets, liabilities and ownership equity are listed as of a specific date, such as the end of its financial year. A balance sheet is often described as a "snapshot of a company's financial condition". Of the four basic financial statements, the balance sheet is the only statement which applies to a single point in time.

A standard company balance sheet has three parts: assets, liabilities and ownership equity. The main categories of assets are usually listed first, and typically in order of liquidity. Assets are followed by the liabilities. The difference between the assets and the liabilities is known as equity or the net assets or the net worth or capital of the company and according to the accounting equation, net worth must equal assets minus liabilities.

Another way to look at the same equation is that assets equals liabilities plus owner's equity. Looking at the equation in this way shows how assets were financed: either by borrowing money (liability) or by using the owner's money (owner's equity). Balance sheets are usually presented with assets in one section and liabilities and net worth in the other section with the two sections "balancing." Records of the values of each account or line in the balance sheet are usually maintained using a system of accounting known as the double-entry bookkeeping system. A business operating entirely in cash can measure its profits by withdrawing the entire bank balance at the end of the period, plus any cash in hand. However, many businesses are not paid immediately; they build up inventories of goods and they acquire buildings and equipment. In other words: businesses have assets and so they can not, even if they want to, immediately turn these into cash at the end of each period. Often, these businesses owe money to suppliers and to tax authorities, and the proprietors do not withdraw all their original capital and profits at the end of each period. In other words businesses also have liabilities.

Origin

It was the Flemish mathematician Simon Stevin who persuaded merchants to make it a rule to summarize accounts at the end of every year in a chapter entitled *Coopmansbouckhouding op de Italiaensche wyse* (Dutch: "Commercial Book-keeping in the Italian Way") of his *Wisconstigheg hedachtenissen* (Dutch: "Mathematical memoirs", Leiden, 1605–08).

Although the balance sheet he required every enterprise to prepare every year was based on entries of the ledger, it was prepared separately from the major books of account. The oldest semi-public balance sheet recorded was that of the East India Company dated 30 April 1671, which was submitted to the company's General Meeting on in 30 August 1671. The publication and audit of the balance sheet was still a rarity in England until the passing of the Bank Charter Act 1844.

Types

A balance sheet summarizes an organization or individual's assets, equity and liabilities at a specific point in time. Individuals and small businesses tend to have simple balance sheets. Larger businesses tend to have more complex balance sheets, and these are presented in the organization's annual report. Large businesses also may prepare balance sheets for segments of their businesses. A balance sheet is often presented alongside one for a different point in time (typically the previous year) for comparison.

Personal Balance Sheet

A personal balance sheet lists current assets such as cash in checking accounts and savings accounts, long-term assets such as common stock and real estate, current liabilities such as loan debt and mortgage debt due, or overdue, long-term liabilities such as mortgage and other loan debt.

Securities and real estate values are listed at market value rather than at historical cost or cost basis. Personal net worth is the difference between an individual's total assets and total liabilities.

US Small Business Balance Sheet

Sample Small Business Balance Sheet

Assets		*Liabilities and Owners' Equity*	
Cash	$6,600	Liabilities	
Accounts Receivable	$6,200	Notes Payable	$30,000
		Accounts Payable	
		Total liabilities	$30,000
Tools and equipment	$25,000	Owners' equity	
		Capital Stock	$7,000
		Retained Earnings	$800
		Total owners' equity	$7,800
Total	$37,800	*Total*	$37,800

A really small business balance sheet lists current assets such as cash, accounts receivable, and inventory, fixed assets such as land, buildings, and equipment, intangible assets such as patents, and liabilities such as accounts payable, accrued expenses, and long-term debt. Contingent liabilities such as warranties are noted in the footnotes to the balance sheet. The small business's equity is the difference between total assets and total liabilities.

Public Business Entities Balance Sheet Structure

Guidelines for balance sheets of public business entities are given by the International Accounting Standards Committee and numerous country-specific organizations. Balance sheet account names and usage depend on the organization's country and the type of organization. Government organizations do not generally follow standards established for individuals or businesses.

If applicable to the business, summary values for the following items should be included on the balance sheet:

Assets

Current assets;

1. Cash and cash equivalents
2. Inventories
3. Accounts receivable
4. Prepaid expenses for future services that will be used within a year.

Fixed assets;

1. Property, plant and equipment
2. Investment property, such as real estate held for investment purposes
3. Intangible assets
4. Financial assets (excluding investments accounted for using the equity method, accounts receivables, and cash and cash equivalents)
5. Investments accounted for using the equity method
6. Biological assets, which are living plants or animals. Bearer biological assets are plants or animals which bear agricultural produce for harvest, such as apple trees grown to produce apples and sheep raised to produce wool.

Liabilities;

1. Accounts payable
2. Provisions for warranties or court decisions
3. Financial liabilities (excluding provisions and accounts payable), such as promissory notes and corporate bonds
4. Liabilities and assets for current tax
5. Deferred tax liabilities and deferred tax assets
6. Minority interest in equity

7. Issued capital and reserves attributable to equity holders of the Parent company
8. Unearned revenue for services paid for by customers but not yet provided.

Equity

The net assets shown by the balance sheet equals the third part of the balance sheet, which is known as the shareholders' equity. Formally, shareholders' equity is part of the company's liabilities: they are funds "owing" to shareholders (after payment of all other liabilities); usually, however, "liabilities" is used in the more restrictive sense of liabilities excluding shareholders' equity. The balance of assets and liabilities (including shareholders' equity) is not a coincidence. Records of the values of each account in the balance sheet are maintained using a system of accounting known as double-entry bookkeeping. In this sense, shareholders' equity by construction must equal assets minus liabilities, and are a residual.

1. Numbers of shares authorized, issued and fully paid, and issued but not fully paid
2. Par value of shares
3. Reconciliation of shares outstanding at the beginning and the end of the period
4. Description of rights, preferences, and restrictions of shares
5. Treasury shares, including shares held by subsidiaries and associates
6. Shares reserved for issuance under options and contracts
7. A description of the nature and purpose of each reserve within owners' equity.

Sample Balance Sheet Structure

The following balance sheet structure is just an example. It does not show all possible kinds of assets, equity and liabilities, but it shows the most usual ones. Because it shows goodwill, it could be a consolidated balance sheet. Monetary values are not shown, summary (total) rows are missing as well.

Income Statement

Income statement, also referred as *profit and loss statement (P&L), earnings statement, operating statement* or *statement of operations*, is a company's financial statement that indicates how the revenue (money received from the sale of products and services before expenses are taken out, also known as the "top line") is transformed into the net income (the result after all revenues and expenses have been accounted for, also known as the "bottom line").

It displays the revenues recognized for a specific period, and the cost and expenses charged against these revenues, including write-offs (e.g., depreciation and amortization of various assets) and taxes. The purpose of the income statement is to show managers and investors whether the company made or lost money during the period being reported.

The important thing to remember about an income statement is that it represents a period of time. This contrasts with the balance sheet, which represents a single moment in time.

Charitable organizations that are required to publish financial statements do not produce an income statement. Instead, they produce a similar statement that reflects funding sources compared against program expenses, administrative costs, and other operating commitments.

This statement is commonly referred to as the statement of activities. Revenues and expenses are further categorized in the statement of activities by the donor restrictions on the funds received and expended.

The income statement can be prepared in one of two methods. The Single Step income statement takes a simpler approach, totaling revenues and subtracting expenses to find the bottom line. The more complex Multi-Step income statement (as the name implies) takes several steps to find the bottom line, starting with the gross profit. It then calculates operating expenses and, when deducted from the gross profit, yields income from operations. Adding to income from operations is the difference of other revenues and other expenses. When combined with income from operations, this yields income before taxes. The final step is to deduct taxes, which finally produces the net income for the period measured.

Usefulness and Limitations of Income Statement

Income statements should help investors and creditors determine the past financial performance of the enterprise, predict future performance, and assess the capability of generating future cash flows through report of the income and expenses. However, information of an income statement has several limitations:

- Items that might be relevant but cannot be reliably measured are not reported (*e.g.* brand recognition and loyalty).
- Some numbers depend on accounting methods used (*e.g.* using FIFO or LIFO accounting to measure inventory level).
- Some numbers depend on judgments and estimates (*e.g.* depreciation expense depends on estimated useful life and salvage value).

Income Statement Bond LLC

For the year ended DECEMBER 31 2007:

	$ Debit	$ Credit
Revenues		
GROSS PROFIT (including rental income)		496,397
Expenses:		
Advertising	6,300	
Bank & credit card fees	144	
Bookkeeping	3,350	
Employees	88,000	
Entertainment	5,550	
Insurance	750	
Legal & professional services	1,575	
Licenses	632	
Printing, postage & stationery	320	
Rent	13,000	
Rental mortgages and fees	74,400	

Telephone	1,000
Utilities	491
Total expenses	(195,512)
Net income	300,885

Items on Income Statement

Operating Section

- Revenue-Cash inflows or other enhancements of assets of an entity during a period from delivering or producing goods, rendering services, or other activities that constitute the entity's ongoing major operations. It is usually presented as sales minus sales discounts, returns, and allowances.
- Expenses-Cash outflows or other using-up of assets or incurrence of liabilities during a period from delivering or producing goods, rendering services, or carrying out other activities that constitute the entity's ongoing major operations.
    - o General and administrative expenses (G & A)-represent expenses to manage the business (officer salaries, legal and professional fees, utilities, insurance, depreciation of office building and equipment, office rents, office supplies)
    - o Selling expenses-represent expenses needed to sell products (*e.g.*, sales salaries, commissions and travel expenses, advertising, freight, shipping, depreciation of sales store buildings and equipment)
    - o Selling General and Administrative expenses (SG&A or SGA)-consist of the combined payroll costs (salaries, commissions, and travel expenses of executives, sales people and employees), and advertising expenses a company incurs. SGA is usually understood as a major portion of non-production related costs, opposing production related costs such as raw material and (direct) labour
    - o R & D expenses-represent expenses included in research and development

- o Depreciation-is the charge for a specific period (*i.e.* year, accounting period) with respect to fixed assets that have been capitalised on the balance sheet.

Non-operating Section

- Other revenues or gains-revenues and gains from other than primary business activities (e.g. rent, patents). It also includes unusual gains and losses that are either unusual or infrequent, but not both (e.g. sale of securities or fixed assets)
- Other expenses or losses-expenses or losses not related to primary business operations.

Irregular Items

They are reported separately because this way users can better predict future cash flows-irregular items most likely will not recur. These are reported net of taxes.

- Discontinued operations is the most common type of irregular items. Shifting business location, stopping production temporarily, or changes due to technological improvement do not qualify as discontinued operations.
- Extraordinary items are both unusual (abnormal) and infrequent, for example, unexpected natural disaster, expropriation, prohibitions under new regulations. Note: natural disaster might not qualify depending on location (e.g. frost damage would not qualify in Canada but would in the tropics).
- Changes in accounting principle is, for example, deciding to depreciate an investment property that has previously not been depreciated. However, changes in estimates (e.g. estimated useful life of a fixed asset) do not qualify.

Earnings Per Share

Because of its importance, earnings per share (EPS) are required to be disclosed on the face of the income statement. A company which reports any of the irregular items must also report EPS for these items either in the statement or in the notes. There are two forms of EPS reported:

- Basic: in this case "weighted average of shares outstanding" includes only actual stocks outstanding.
- Diluted: in this case "weighted average of shares outstanding" is calculated as if all stock options, warrants, convertible bonds, and other securities that could be transformed into shares *are* transformed. This increases the number of shares and so EPS decreases. Diluted EPS is considered to be a more reliable way to measure EPS.

Family Fitness and Fun

Statements of Income

Revenues	$12,580.2	$ 10,900.4	$ 8,290.3
Cost of sales	6,740.2	5,650.1	4,524.2
Gross profit	6,835.0	5,657.3	3,270.1
Selling, general and administrative expenses	3,624.6	3,296.3	3,034.0
Other (income) expense, net	1,100.3	(20.0)	18.0
Operating profit	2,122.1	2,166.0	2,013.1
Interest expense, net	119.7	124.1	142.8
Income before income taxes	2,102.4	1,980.9	1,870.3
Provision for income taxes	680.3	620.6	582.0

Net income $ 1,720.1 $ 1,421.3 $ 1,190.3

Viacom Inc. And Subsidiaries

Consolidated Statements of Operations

			(In millions)
Year Ended December 31,	*2004*	*2003*	*2002*
Revenues	$ 22,525.9	$ 20,827.6	$19,186.8
Expenses:			
Operating	12,545.8	11,879.8	10,735.5
Selling, general and administrative	4,142.1	3,732.3	3,498.6
Depreciation and amortization	809.9	741.9	711.8
Impairment charge (Note 3)	17,997.1	—	—
Total expenses	35,494.9	16,354.0	14,945.9

Operating income (loss)	(12,969.0)	4,473.6	4,240.9
Interest expense	(718.9)	(742.9)	(799.1)
Interest income	25.3	11.7	12.0
Other items, net	7.6	(3.0)	(32.9)
Earnings (loss) from continuing operations before income taxes, equity in earnings (loss) of affiliated companies and minority interest	(13,655.0)	3,739.4	3,420.9
Provision for income taxes	(1,378.6)	(1,497.0)	(1,338.3)
Equity in earnings (loss) of affiliated companies, net of tax	(20.8)	.1	(37.3)
Minority interest, net of tax	(5.1)	(4.7)	(3.3)
Net Income (loss) from continuing operations	(15,059.5)	2,237.8	2,042.0
Discontinued operations (Note 2):			
Earnings (loss) from discontinued operations	(1,182.7)	(718.8)	255.3
Income taxes, net of minority interest	92.4	(83.6)	(90.7)
Net Income (loss) from discontinued operations	(1,090.3)	(802.4)	164.6
Net Income (loss) before cumulative effect of accounting change	(16,149.8)	1,435.4	2,206.6
Cumulative effect of accounting change, net of minority interest and tax (Note 1)	(1,312.4)	(18.5)	(1,480.9)
Net Income (loss)	$ (17,462.2)	$ 1,416.9	$ 725.7

Bottom Line

"Bottom line" is the net income that is calculated after subtracting the expenses from revenue. Since this forms the last line of the income statement, it is informally called "bottom line." It is important to investors as it represents the profit for the year attributable to the shareholders.

Cash Flow Statement

In financial accounting, a cash flow statement, also known as *statement of cash flows* or *funds flow statement*, is a financial statement that shows how changes in balance sheet accounts and income affect cash and cash equivalents, and breaks the analysis down to operating, investing, and financing activities. Essentially, the cash flow statement is concerned with the flow of cash in and cash out of the business. The statement captures both the current operating results and the accompanying changes in the balance sheet. As an analytical tool, the statement of cash flows is useful in determining the short-term viability of a company, particularly its ability to pay bills. International Accounting Standard 7 (IAS 7), is the International Accounting Standard that deals with cash flow statements.

People and groups interested in cash flow statements include:

- Accounting personnel, who need to know whether the organization will be able to cover payroll and other immediate expenses
- Potential lenders or creditors, who want a clear picture of a company's ability to repay
- Potential investors, who need to judge whether the company is financially sound
- Potential employees or contractors, who need to know whether the company will be able to afford compensation
- Shareholders of the business.

Purpose

The cash flow statement was previously known as the flow of funds statement. The cash flow statement reflects a firm's liquidity.

The balance sheet is a snapshot of a firm's financial resources and obligations at a single point in time, and the income statement summarizes a firm's financial transactions over an interval of time. These two financial statements reflect the accrual basis accounting used by firms to match revenues with the expenses associated with generating those revenues.

The cash flow statement includes only inflows and outflows of cash and cash equivalents; it excludes transactions that do not directly affect cash receipts and payments. These noncash transactions include depreciation or write-offs on bad debts or credit losses to name a few. The cash flow statement is a cash basis report on three types of financial activities: operating activities, investing activities, and financing activities. Noncash activities are usually reported in footnotes.

The cash flow statement is intended to

1. provide information on a firm's liquidity and solvency and its ability to change cash flows in future circumstances
2. provide additional information for evaluating changes in assets, liabilities and equity
3. improve the comparability of different firms' operating performance by eliminating the effects of different accounting methods
4. indicate the amount, timing and probability of future cash flows.

The cash flow statement has been adopted as a standard financial statement because it eliminates allocations, which might be derived from different accounting methods, such as various timeframes for depreciating fixed assets.

History and Variations

Cash basis financial statements were common before accrual basis financial statements. The "flow of funds" statements of the past were cash flow statements.

In 1863, the Dowlais Iron Company had receovered from a business slump, but had no cash to invest for a new blast furnace, despite having made a profit. To explain why there were no funds to invest, the manager made a new financial statement that was called a *comparison balance sheet,* which showed that the company was holding too much inventory. This new financial statement was the genesis of Cash Flow Statement that is used today.

In the United States in 1971, the Financial Accounting Standards Board (FASB) defined rules that made it mandatory under

Generally Accepted Accounting Principles (US GAAP) to report sources and uses of funds, but the definition of "funds" was not clear." Net working capital" might be cash or might be the difference between current assets and current liabilities. From the late 1970 to the mid-1980s, the FASB discussed the usefulness of predicting future cash flows. In 1987, FASB Statement No. 95 (FAS 95) mandated that firms provide cash flow statements. In 1992, the International Accounting Standards Board issued International Accounting Standard 7 (IAS 7), *Cash Flow Statements*, which became effective in 1994, mandating that firms provide cash flow statements. US GAAP and IAS 7 rules for cash flow statements are similar. Differences include:

- IAS 7 requires that the cash flow statement include changes in both cash and cash equivalents. US GAAP permits using cash alone or cash and cash equivalents.
- IAS 7 permits bank borrowings (overdraft) in certain countries to be included in cash equivalents rather than being considered a part of financing activities.
- IAS 7 allows interest paid to be included in operating activities or financing activities. US GAAP requires that interest paid be included in operating activities.
- US GAAP (FAS 95) requires that when the direct method is used to present the operating activities of the cash flow statement, a supplemental schedule must also present a cash flow statement using the indirect method. The IASC strongly recommends the direct method but allows either method. The IASC considers the indirect method less clear to users of financial statements. Cash flow statements are most commonly prepared using the indirect method, which is not especially useful in projecting future cash flows.

Cash Flow Activities

The cash flow statement is partitioned into three segments, namely: cash flow resulting from operating activities, cash flow resulting from investing activities, and cash flow resulting from financing activities. The money coming into the business is called cash inflow, and money going out from the business is called cash outflow.

Operating Activities

Operating activities include the production, sales and delivery of the company's product as well as collecting payment from its customers.

This could include purchasing raw materials, building inventory, advertising, and shipping the product.

Under IAS 7, operating cash flows include:

- Receipts from the sale of goods or services
- Receipts for the sale of loans, debt or equity instruments in a trading portfolio
- Interest received on loans
- Dividends received on equity securities
- Payments to suppliers for goods and services
- Payments to employees or on behalf of employees
- Interest payments (alternatively, this can be reported under financing activities in IAS 7, and US GAAP).

Items which are added back to [or subtracted from, as appropriate] the net income figure (which is found on the Income Statement) to arrive at cash flows from operations generally include:

- Depreciation (loss of tangible asset value over time)
- Deferred tax
- Amortization (loss of intangible asset value over time)
- Any gains or losses associated with the sale of a non-current asset, because associated cash flows do not belong in the operating section. (unrealized gains/losses are also added back from the income statement).

Investing Activities

Examples of Investing activities are

- Purchase of an asset (assets can be land, building, equipment, marketable securities, etc.)

- Loans made to suppliers or customers
- Payments related to mergers and acquisitions.

Financing Activities

Financing activities include the inflow of cash from investors such as banks and shareholders, as well as the outflow of cash to shareholders as dividends as the company generates income. Other activities which impact the long-term liabilities and equity of the company are also listed in the financing activities section of the cash flow statement.

Under IAS 7;

- Proceeds from issuing short-term or long-term debt
- Payments of dividends
- Payments for repurchase of company shares
- Repayment of debt principal, including capital leases
- For non-profit organizations, receipts of donor-restricted cash that is limited to long-term purposes.

Items under the financing activities section include:

- Dividends paid
- Sale or repurchase of the company's stock
- Net borrowings
- Payment of dividend tax.

Disclosure of Noncash Activities

Under IAS 7, noncash investing and financing activities are disclosed in footnotes to the financial statements.

Under US General Accepted Accounting Principles (GAAP), noncash activities may be disclosed in a footnote or within the cash flow statement itself. Noncash financing activities may include

- Leasing to purchase an asset
- Converting debt to equity
- Exchanging noncash assets or liabilities for other noncash assets or liabilities
- Issuing shares in exchange for assets.

Preparation Methods

The direct method of preparing a cash flow statement results in a more easily understood report. The indirect method is almost universally used, because FAS 95 requires a supplementary report similar to the indirect method if a company chooses to use the direct method.

Direct Method

The direct method for creating a cash flow statement reports major classes of gross cash receipts and payments. Under IAS 7, dividends received may be reported under operating activities or under investing activities. If taxes paid are directly linked to operating activities, they are reported under operating activities; if the taxes are directly linked to investing activities or financing activities, they are reported under investing or financing activities.

Sample cash flow statement using the direct method :

Cash flows from (used in) operating activities	
Cash receipts from customers	27,500
Cash paid to suppliers and employees	(20,000)
Cash generated from operations (sum)	7,500
Interest paid	(2,000)
Income taxes paid	(4,000)
Net cash flows from operating activities	1,500
Cash flows from (used in) investing activities	
Proceeds from the sale of equipment	7,500
Dividends received	3,000
Net cash flows from investing activities	10,500
Cash flows from (used in) financing	
activities Dividends paid	(2,500)
Net cash flows used in financing activities	(2,500).
Net increase in cash and cash equivalents	9,500
Cash and cash equivalents, beginning of year	1,000
Cash and cash equivalents, end of year	$10,500

Indirect Method

The indirect method uses net-income as a starting point, makes adjustments for all transactions for non-cash items, then adjusts for all cash-based transactions. An increase in an asset account is subtracted from net income, and an increase in a liability account is added back to net income. This method converts accrual-basis net income (or loss) into cash flow by using a series of additions and deductions.

Rules

The following rules are used to make adjustments for changes in current assets and liabilities, operating items not providing or using cash and nonoperating items.

- Likami
- Increase in non-cash current asset are subtracted from net income
- Increase in current liabilities are added to net income
- Decrease in current liabilities are subtracted from net income
- Expenses with no cash outflows are added back to net income (depreciation and/or amortization expense are the only operating items that have no effect on cash flows in the period)
- Revenues with no cash inflows are subtracted from net income
- Non operating losses are added back to net income
- Non operating gains are subtracted from net income.

Example: cash flow of Citigroup:

Citigroup Cash Flow Statement (all numbers in millions of US$)

Period ending	*12/31/2007*	*12/31/2006*	*12/31/2005*
Net income	21,538	24,589	17,046
Operating activities, cash flows provided by or used in:			
Depreciation and amortization	2,790	2,592	2,747
Adjustments to net income	4,617	621	2,910

Decrease (increase) in accounts receivable	12,503	17,236	—
Increase (decrease) in liabilities (A/P, taxes payable)	131,622	19,822	37,856
Decrease (increase) in inventories	—	—	—
Increase (decrease) in other operating activities	(173,057)	(33,061)	(62,963)
Net cash flow from operating activities	13	31,799	(2,404)
Investing activities, cash flows provided by or used in:			
Capital expenditures	(4,035)	(3,724)	(3,011)
Investments	(201,777)	(71,710)	(75,649)
Other cash flows from investing activities	1,606	17,009	(571)
Net cash flows from investing activities	(204,206)	(58,425)	(79,231)
Financing activities, cash flows provided by or used in:			
Dividends paid	(9,826)	(9,188)	(8,375)
Sale (repurchase) of stock	(5,327)	(12,090)	133
Increase (decrease) in debt	101,122	26,651	21,204
Other cash flows from financing activities	120,461	27,910	70,349
Net cash flows from financing activities	206,430	33,283	83,311
Effect of exchange rate changes	645	(1,840)	731
Net increase (decrease) in cash and cash equivalents	2,882	4,817	2,407

Equity (Finance)

In accounting and finance, equity is the residual claim or interest of the most junior class of investors in assets, after all liabilities are paid. If valuations placed on assets do not exceed liabilities, negative equity exists. In an accounting context,

Shareholders' equity (or stockholders' equity, shareholders' funds, shareholders' capital or similar terms) represents the remaining interest in assets of a company, spread among individual shareholders of common or preferred stock.

At the start of a business, owners put some funding into the business to finance assets. This creates liability on the business in the shape of capital as the business is a separate entity from its owners. Businesses can be considered to be, for accounting purposes, sums of liabilities and assets; this is the accounting equation. After liabilities have been accounted for, the positive remainder is deemed the owner's interest in the business.

This definition is helpful to understand the liquidation process in case of bankruptcy. At first, all the secured creditors are paid against proceeds from assets. Afterward, a series of creditors, ranked in priority sequence, have the next claim/right on the residual proceeds. Ownership equity is the last or residual claim against assets, paid only after all other creditors are paid. In such cases where even creditors could not get enough money to pay their bills, and nothing is left over to reimburse owners' equity. Thus owners' equity is reduced to zero. Ownership equity is also known as risk capital, liable capital and equity.

Equity Investments

Equity investments generally refers to the buying and holding of shares of stock on a stock market by individuals and firms in anticipation of income from dividends and capital gain as the value of the stock rises. It also sometimes refers to the acquisition of equity (ownership) participation in a private (unlisted) company or a startup (a company being created or newly created). When the investment is in infant companies, it is referred to as venture capital investing and is generally understood to be higher risk than investment in listed going-concern situations.

The equities held by private individuals are often held via mutual funds or other forms of pooled investment vehicle, many of which have quoted prices that are listed in financial newspapers or magazines; the mutual funds are typically managed by prominent fund management firms (e.g. Schroders, Fidelity

Investments or the Vanguard Group). Such holdings allow individual investors to obtain the diversification of the fund(s) and to obtain the skill of the professional fund managers in charge of the fund(s). An alternative, usually employed by large private investors and pension funds, is to hold shares directly; in the institutional environment many clients who own portfolios have what are called segregated funds as opposed to, or in addition to, the pooled e.g. mutual fund alternative.

A calculation can be made to assess whether an equity is over or underpriced compared with a long-term government bond. This is called the Yield Gap or Yield Ratio. It is the ratio of the dividend yield of an equity and that of the long-term bond.

Accounting

In financial accounting, it is the owners' interest on the assets of the enterprise after deducting all its liabilities. It appears on the balance sheet/Statement of Financial Position, one of the four primary financial statements.

Ownership equity includes both tangible and intangible items (such as brand names and reputation/goodwill).

Accounts listed under ownership equity include (example):

- Preferred stock
- Share capital, common stock
- Capital surplus
- Stock options
- Retained earnings
- Treasury stock
- Reserve (accounting).

Book Value

The book value of equity will change in the case of the following events:

- Changes in the firm's assets relative to its liabilities. For example, a profitable firm receives more cash for its products than the cost at which it produced these goods, and so in the act of making a profit it is increasing its assets.

- Depreciation. Equity will decrease, for example, when machinery depreciates, which is registered as a decline in the value of the asset, and on the liabilities side of the firm's balance sheet as a decrease in shareholders' equity.
- Issue of new equity in which the firm obtains new capital increases the total shareholders' equity.
- Share repurchases, in which a firm gives back money to its investors, reducing on the asset side its financial assets, and on the liability side the shareholders' equity. For practical purposes (except for its tax consequences), share repurchasing is similar to a dividend payment, as both consist of the firm giving money back to investors. Rather than giving money to all shareholders immediately in the form of a dividend payment, a share repurchase reduces the number of shares (increases the size of each share) in future income and distributions.
- Dividends paid out to preferred stock owners are considered an expense to be subtracted from net income (from the point of view of the common share owners).
- Other reasons. Assets and liabilities can change without any effect being measured in the Income Statement under certain circumstances; for example, changes in accounting rules may be applied retroactively. Sometimes assets bought and held in other countries get translated back into the reporting currency at different exchange rates, resulting in a changed value.

Shareholders' Equity

When the owners are shareholders, the interest can be called shareholders' equity; the accounting remains the same, and it is ownership equity spread out among shareholders. If all shareholders are in one and the same class, they share equally in ownership equity from all perspectives. However, shareholders may allow different priority ranking among themselves by the use of share classes, and options. This complicates both analysis for stock valuation, and accounting. The individual investor is interested not only in the total changes to equity, but also in the increase/decrease in the value of his own personal share of the equity. This reconciliation of equity should be done both in total and on a per share basis.

- Equity (beg. of year)
- + net income inter net money you gained
- " dividends how much money you gained or lost so far
- +/" gain/loss from changes to the number of shares outstanding.more or less
- = Equity (end of year) if you get more money during the year or less or not anything.

Market Value of Shares

In the stock market, market price per share does not correspond to the equity per share calculated in the accounting statements. Stock valuations, often much higher, are based on other considerations related to the business' operating cashflow, profits and future prospects; some factors are derived from the accounting statements. Thus, there is little or no correlation between the equity seen in financial statements and the stock valuation of the business.

Real Estate Equity

Individuals can also use market valuations to calculate equity in real estate. An owner refers to his or her equity in a property as the difference between the market price of a property and the liability attached to the property (mortgage or home equity loan).

Statement of Retained Earnings

The Statement of Retained Earnings (also known as Equity Statement, Statement of Owner's Equity for a single proprietorship, Statement of Partner's Equity for partnership, and Statement of Retained Earnings and Stockholders' Equity for corporation) is one of the basic financial statements as per Generally Accepted Accounting Principles, and it explains the changes in a company's retained earnings over the reporting period. It breaks down changes affecting the account, such as profits or losses from operations, dividends paid, and any other items charged or credited to retained earnings. A retained earnings statement is required by Generally Accepted Accounting Principles (GAAP) whenever comparative balance sheets and income statements are presented. It may appear in the balance sheet, in a combined income statement and changes in retained earnings statement, or as a separate schedule.

Therefore, the statement of retained earnings uses information from the income statement and provides information to the balance sheet. Retained earnings are part of the balance sheet (another basic financial statement) under "stockholders equity," and is mostly affected by net income earned during a period of time by the company less any dividends paid to the company's owners/ stockholders. The retained earnings account on the balance sheet is said to represent an "accumulation of earnings" since net profits and losses are added/subtracted from the account from period to period. The general equation can be expressed as following:

Ending Retained Earnings = Beginning Retained Earnings-Dividends Paid + Net Income.

Generally Accepted Auditing Standards

Generally Accepted Auditing Standards, or GAAS are sets of standards against which the quality of audits may be judged. Several organizations have developed such sets of principles, which vary by territory.

US GAAS

US GAAS are ten auditing standards, developed by the American Institute of Certified Public Accountants, consisting of general standards, standards of field work, and standards of reporting, along with interpretations. They were developed by the AICPA in 1947 and have undergone minor changes since then.

The US GAAS are as follows:

General Standards

1. The auditor must have adequate technical training and proficiency to perform the audit.

2. The auditor must maintain independence in mental attitude in all matters related to the audit.
3. The auditor must use due professional care during the performance of the audit and the preparation of the report.

ISAs

International Standards on Auditing are developed by the International Auditing and Assurance Standards Board of the International Federation of Accountants. Derivatives of ISAs are used in the audit of several other juristictions, including the United Kingdom.

Internal Audit

Internal auditing is a profession and activity involved in helping organizations achieve their stated objectives. It does this by using a systematic methodology for analysing business processes, procedures and activities with the goal of highlighting organizational problems and recommending solutions. Professionals called internal auditors are employed by organizations to perform the internal auditing activity.

The scope of internal auditing within an organization is broad and may involve topics such as the efficacy of operations, the reliability of financial reporting, deterring and investigating fraud, safeguarding assets, and compliance with laws and regulations.

Internal auditing frequently involves measuring compliance with the entity's policies and procedures. However, Internal auditors are not responsible for the execution of company activities; they advise management and the Board of Directors (or similar oversight body) regarding how to better execute their responsibilities. As a result of their broad scope of involvement, internal auditors may have a variety of higher educational and professional backgrounds.

Publicly-traded corporations typically have an internal auditing department, led by a Chief Audit Executive ("CAE") who generally reports to the Audit Committee of the Board of Directors, with administrative reporting to the Chief Executive Officer. The profession is unregulated, though there are a number of international standard setting bodies, an example of which is the Institute of Internal Auditors ("IIA"). The IIA has established Standards for the Professional Practice of Internal Auditing and has over 150,000 members representing 165 countries, including approximately 65,000 Certified Internal Auditors.

History of Internal Auditing

The Internal Auditing profession evolved steadily with the progress of management science after World War II. It is conceptually similar in many ways to financial auditing by public accounting firms, quality assurance and banking compliance activities. Much of the theory underlying internal auditing is derived from management consulting and public accounting professions. With the implementation in the United States of the Sarbanes-Oxley Act of 2002, the profession's growth accelerated, as many internal auditors possess the skills required to help companies meet the requirements of the law.

Organizational Independence

To perform their role effectively, internal auditors require organizational independence from management, to enable unrestricted evaluation of management activities and personnel. Although internal auditors are part of company management and paid by the company, the primary customer of internal audit activity is the entity charged with oversight of management's activities. This is typically the Audit Committee, a subcommittee of the Board of Directors. To provide independence, most Chief Audit Executives report to the Chairperson of the Audit Committee and can only be replaced with the concurrence of that individual.

Role in Internal Control

Internal auditing activity is primarily directed at improving internal control. Under the COSO Framework, internal control is broadly defined as a process, effected by an entity's board of directors, management, and other personnel, designed to provide reasonable assurance regarding the achievement of objectives in the following internal control categories:

- Effectiveness and efficiency of operations.

- Reliability of financial reporting.
- Compliance with laws and regulations.

Management is responsible for internal control. Managers establish policies and processes to help the organization achieve specific objectives in each of these categories. Internal auditors perform audits to evaluate whether the policies and processes are designed and operating effectively and provide recommendations for improvement.

In the United States, internal auditors may assist management with compliance with the Sarbanes-Oxley Act (SOX).

Role in Risk Management

Internal auditing professional standards require the function to monitor and evaluate the effectiveness of the organization's Risk management processes. Risk management relates to how an organization sets objectives, then identifies, analyses, and responds to those risks that could potentially impact its ability to realize its objectives.

Under the COSO enterprise risk management (ERM) Framework, risks fall under strategic, operational, financial reporting, and legal/regulatory categories. Management performs risk assessment activities as part of the ordinary course of business in each of these categories. Examples include: strategic planning, marketing planning, capital planning, budgeting, hedging, incentive payout structure, and credit/lending practices. Sarbanes-Oxley regulations also require extensive risk assessment of financial reporting processes. Corporate legal counsel often prepares comprehensive assessments of the current and potential litigation a company faces. Internal auditors may evaluate each of these activities, or focus on the processes used by management to report and monitor the risks identified. For example, internal auditors can advise management regarding the reporting of forward-looking operating measures to the Board, to help identify emerging risks.

In larger organizations, major strategic initiatives are implemented to achieve objectives and drive changes. As a member of senior management, the Chief Audit Executive (CAE) may participate in status updates on these major initiatives. This places the CAE in the position to report on many of the major risks the organization faces to the Audit Committee, or ensure management's reporting is effective for that purpose.

Internal auditors may help companies establish and maintain Enterprise Risk Management processes. Internal auditors also play an important role in helping companies execute a SOX 404 top-down risk assessment. In these latter two areas, internal auditors typically are part of the project team in an advisory role.

Role in Corporate Governance

Internal auditing activity as it relates to corporate governance is generally informal, accomplished primarily through participation in meetings and discussions with members of the Board of Directors. Corporate governance is a combination of processes and organizational structures implemented by the Board of Directors to inform, direct, manage, and monitor the organization's resources, strategies and policies towards the achievement of the organizations objectives. The internal auditor is often considered one of the "four pillars" of corporate governance, the other pillars being the Board of Directors, management, and the external auditor.

A primary focus area of internal auditing as it relates to corporate governance is helping the Audit Committee of the Board of Directors (or equivalent) perform its responsibilities effectively. This may include reporting critical internal control problems, informing the Committee privately on the capabilities of key managers, suggesting questions or topics for the Audit Committee's meeting agendas, and coordinating carefully with the external auditor and management to ensure the Committee receives effective information.

Nature of the Internal Audit Activity

Based on a risk assessment of the organization, internal auditors, management and oversight Boards determine where to focus internal auditing efforts. Internal auditing activity is generally conducted as one or more discrete projects. A typical internal audit project involves the following steps:

1. Establish and communicate the scope and objectives for the audit to appropriate management.

2. Develop an understanding of the business area under review. This includes objectives, measurements, and key transaction types. This involves review of documents and interviews. Flowcharts and narratives may be created if necessary.
3. Describe the key risks facing the business activities within the scope of the audit.
4. Identify control procedures used to ensure each key risk and transaction type is properly controlled and monitored.
5. Develop and execute a risk-based sampling and testing approach to determine whether the most important controls are operating as intended.
6. Report problems identified and negotiate action plans with management to address the problems.
7. Follow-up on reported findings at appropriate intervals. Internal audit departments maintain a follow-up database for this purpose.

Project length varies based on the complexity of the activity being audited and Internal Audit resources available. Many of the above steps are iterative and may not all occur in the sequence indicated.

By analysing and recommending business improvements in critical areas, auditors help the organization meet its objectives. In addition to assessing business processes, specialists called Information Technology (IT) Auditors review information technology controls.

Developing the Plan of Engagements

Internal auditing standards require the development of a plan of audit engagements (projects) based on a risk assessment, updated at least annually. The input of senior management and the Board is typically included in this process. Many departments update their plan of engagements throughout the year as risks or organizational priorities change. This effort helps ensure the audit activity is aligned with the organization's objectives, by answering two key questions: First, what goals are the organization trying to accomplish in the upcoming period? Second, how can the Internal Audit Department assist the organization in achieving these goals?

Internal auditors often conduct a series of interviews of senior management to identify potential engagements. Changes in people, processes, or systems often generate audit project ideas. Various documents are reviewed, such as strategic plans, financial reports, consulting studies, etc.

Further, the results of prior audits and resolution of open issues are considered. For example, even if a business area is important, prior audit work and the nature and status of open issues may render further audit effort unnecessary. If the organization has a formal enterprise risk management (ERM) program, the risks identified therein help limit the amount of separate risk assessment performed by Internal Audit.

The preliminary plan of engagements is documented and prioritized. Audit resources and expertise are then considered and a final plan is presented to senior management and the Audit Committee. The presentations vary based on the needs of the stakeholders and may include the following:

- Summary of key goals, risks and corresponding major audits, to illustrate alignment;
- Analyses of audit effort along a variety of dimensions (e.g., by business segment, COSO objective category, IT, Sarbanes-Oxley, vs. prior year, etc.) along with commentary regarding changes;
- Brief description of critical projects identified;
- Projects requested but not planned for execution due to prioritization and resources;
- Required co-sourcing effort, typically where outside expertise is required or during peak periods;
- Coordination with other risk functions, such as legal, compliance or insurance, to ensure coverage of key organizational risks;
- Update on audit staffing levels, experience and certification; and

- Appendix materials, such as planning approach, assumptions (e.g., days per auditor and staffing level) and brief descriptions of all planned audits and related prioritization.

Best Practices in Internal Auditing

Measuring the Internal Audit Function

The measurement of the internal audit function can involve a balanced scorecard approach. Internal audit functions are primarily evaluated based on the quality of counsel and information provided to the Audit Committee and top management. However, this is primarily qualitative and therefore difficult to measure. "Customer surveys" sent to key managers after each audit project or report can be used to measure performance, with an annual survey to the Audit Committee. Scoring on dimensions such as professionalism, quality of counsel, timeliness of work product, utility of meetings, and quality of status updates are typical with such surveys. Understanding the expectations of senior management and the audit committee represent important steps in developing a performance measurement process, as well as how such measures help align the audit function with organizational priorities.

Quantitative measures can also be used to measure the function's level of execution and qualifications of its personnel. Key measures include:

Plan completion: This is a measure of the degree to which the annual plan of engagements is completed, measured at a point in time. This may be measured using the number of projects completed, weighted by the planned size of each project, with estimates for projects in-progress. Measured throughout the year, it is compared against the percentage of the year elapsed.

Report issuance: This is a measure of the time elapsed from completion of testing to issuance of the final audit report, including management's action plans. This can be measured in average days or percentage of reports issued within a certain standard, such as 30 days. Establishing expectations for the timing of management's response to report recommendations is critical. In addition, the scope and degree of change involved in the report's action plans are key variables. For example, a report for a single retail store requiring only the store manager's action might take 3–5 days to issue. However, a report consolidating findings from 20 retail stores, with action plans with national implications determined by top management, may take 30–60 days in complex organizations.

Issue closure: Reported audit findings are often called "issues" or "deficiencies." Professional standards require audit functions to track reported findings to resolution, which effectively requires the maintenance of an issues follow-up database. The number of days that reported issues remain open, or open after their agreed-upon closure date, are key measures. In addition, reporting database statistics such as the number of issues open (unresolved), closed (resolved), and issues opened/closed during a given period are useful statistics.

Staff qualifications: This can be measured through the percentage of staff with professional certifications, graduate degrees, and overall years of experience.

Staff utilization rate: This is measured as the percentage of time spent on projects, as opposed to administrative time such as training or vacation. Many internal audit departments track time by audit project. This is typically captured in a database or spreadsheet.

Staffing level: The number of positions filled relative to the authorized staffing level. Due to the challenge of finding qualified staff, departments may have rotational programs to bring in management to complete tours in the function or be "guest" auditors. Audit departments also "co-source," meaning they obtain contract auditors from service providers.

Developing and Retaining Staff

Developing and retaining quality professionals is a key concern in the profession. Key methods for developing and retaining internal audit staff personnel include:

- Providing challenging, varied assignments
- Ensuring quality supervision

- Ensuring staff participates in projects from start to finish, to learn all phases of the audit process
- Providing opportunities to lead (in-charge) projects, starting with more structured projects such as Sarbanes-Oxley work
- Participating on departmental improvement task forces, such as preparation for quality assurance review
- Participating in the recruiting and interviewing process for new hires
- Rotating through various audit teams (in larger departments) or audits of various businesses
- Providing both outside training (e.g., seminars) and in-house training (e.g., company systems) for two weeks/ year
- Participation in annual risk assessment activities, whether asking key questions or just taking notes.

Reporting of Critical Findings

The Chief Audit Executive (CAE) typically reports the most critical issues to the Audit Committee quarterly, along with management's progress towards resolving them. Critical issues typically have a reasonable likelihood of causing substantial financial or reputational damage to the company. For particularly complex issues, the responsible manager may participate in the discussion. Such reporting is critical to ensure the function is respected, that the proper "tone at the top" exists in the organization, and to expedite resolution of such issues. It is a matter of considerable judgment to select appropriate issues for the Audit Committee's attention and to describe them in the proper context.

6

Working Capital Management of Hospitality Industry

Financial management entails planning for the future of a person or a business enterprise to ensure a positive cash flow. It includes the administration and maintenance of financial assets. Besides, financial management covers the process of identifying and managing risks.

The primary concern of financial management is the assessment rather than the techniques of financial quantification. A financial manager looks at the available data to judge the performance of enterprises. Managerial finance is an interdisciplinary approach that borrows from both managerial accounting and corporate finance.

Some experts refer to financial management as the science of money management. The primary usage of this term is in the world of financing business activities. However, financial management is important at all levels of human existence because every entity needs to look after its finances.

Financial Management: Levels

Broadly speaking, the process of financial management takes place at two levels. At the individual level, financial management involves tailoring expenses according to the financial resources of an individual. Individuals with surplus cash or access to funding invest their money to make up for the impact of taxation and inflation. Else, they spend it on discretionary items. They need to be able to take the financial decisions that are intended to benefit them in the long run and help them achieve their financial goals.

From an organizational point of view, the process of financial management is associated with financial planning and financial control. Financial planning seeks to quantify various financial resources available and plan the size and timing of expenditures. Financial control refers to monitoring cash flow. Inflow is the amount of money coming into a particular company, while outflow is a record of the expenditure being made by the company. Managing this movement of funds in relation to the budget is essential for a business.

At the corporate level, the main aim of the process of managing finances is to achieve the various goals a company sets at a given point of time. Businesses also seek to generate substantial amounts of profits, following a particular set of financial processes.

Financial managers aim to boost the levels of resources at their disposal. Besides, they control the functioning on money put in by external investors. Providing investors with sufficient amount of returns on their investments is one of the goals that every company tries to achieve. Efficient financial management ensures that this becomes possible.

Strong financial management in the business arena requires managers to be able to:

1. Interpret financial reports including income statements, Profits and Loss or P&L, cash flow statements and balance sheet statements
2. Improve the allocation of working capital within business operations
3. Review and fine tune financial budgeting, and revenue and cost forecasting
4. Look at the funding options for business expansion, including both long and short term financing
5. Review the financial health of the company or business unit using ratio analyses, such as the gearing ratio, profit per employee and weighted cost of capital

6. Understand the various techniques using in project and asset valuations
7. Apply critical financial decision making techniques to assess whether to proceed with an investment
8. Understand valuations frameworks for businesses, portfolios and intangible assets

Managerial Finance

Managerial finance is the branch of the finance that concerns itself with the managerial significance of finance techniques. It is focused on assessment rather than technique.

The difference between a managerial and a technical approach can be seen in the questions one might ask of annual reports. One concerned with technique would be primarily interested in measurement. They would ask: are moneys being assigned to the right categories? Were generally accepted accounting principles GAAP followed?

One concerned with management though would want to know what the figures mean.

- They might compare the returns to other businesses in their industry and ask: are we performing better or worse than our peers? If so, what is the source of the problem? Do we have the same profit margins? If not why? Do we have the same expenses? Are we paying more for something than our peers?
- They may look at changes in asset balances looking for red flags that indicate problems with bill collection or bad debt.
- They will analyse working capital to anticipate future cash flow problems.

Managerial finance is an interdisciplinary approach that borrows from both managerial accounting and corporate finance.

Sound financial management creates value and organisational agility through the allocation of scarce resources amongst competing business opportunities. It is an aid to the implementation and monitoring of business strategies and helps achieve business objectives.

The Role of Managerial Accounting

To interpret financial results in the manner described above, managers use Financial analysis techniques. Managers also need to look at how resources are allocated within an organization. They need to know what each activity costs and why. These questions require managerial accounting techniques such as activity based costing.

Managers also need to anticipate future expenses. To get a better understanding of the accuracy of the budgeting process, they may use variable budgeting.

The Role of Corporate Finance

Managerial finance is also interested in determining the best way to use money to improve future opportunities to earn money and minimize the impact of financial shocks. To accomplish these goals managerial finance uses the following techniques borrowed from Corporate finance:

- Valuation
- Portfolio theory
- Hedging
- Capital structure.

Corporate Finance

Corporate finance is an area of finance dealing with financial decisions business enterprises make and the tools and analysis used to make these decisions. The primary goal of corporate finance is to maximize corporate value while managing the firm's financial risks. Although it is in principle different from managerial finance which studies the financial decisions of all firms, rather than corporations alone, the main concepts in the study of corporate finance are applicable to the financial problems of all kinds of firms.

The discipline can be divided into long-term and short-term decisions and techniques. Capital investment decisions are long-term choices about which projects receive investment, whether to finance that investment with equity or debt, and when or whether to pay dividends to shareholders. On the other hand, the short term decisions can be grouped under the heading "Working capital management". This subject deals with the short-term balance of current assets and current liabilities; the focus here is on managing cash, inventories, and short-term borrowing and lending (such as the terms on credit extended to customers).

The terms corporate finance and corporate financier are also associated with investment banking. The typical role of an investment bank is to evaluate the company's financial needs and raise the appropriate type of capital that best fits those needs.

Capital Investment Decisions

Capital investment decisions are long-term corporate finance decisions relating to fixed assets and capital structure. Decisions are based on several inter-related criteria. (1) Corporate management seeks to maximize the value of the firm by investing in projects which yield a positive net present value when valued using an appropriate discount rate. (2) These projects must also be financed appropriately. (3) If no such opportunities exist, maximizing shareholder value dictates that management must return excess cash to shareholders (i.e., distribution via dividends). Capital investment decisions thus comprise an investment decision, a financing decision, and a dividend decision.

The Investment Decision

Management must allocate limited resources between competing opportunities (projects) in a process known as capital budgeting. Making this capital allocation decision requires estimating the value of each opportunity or project, which is a function of the size, timing and predictability of future cash flows.

Project Valuation

In general, each project's value will be estimated using a discounted cash flow (DCF) valuation, and the opportunity with the highest value, as measured by the resultant net present value (NPV) will be selected. This requires estimating the size and timing of all of the incremental cash flows resulting from the project. Such future cash flows are then discounted to determine their *present value*. These present values are then summed, and this sum net of the initial investment outlay is the NPV.

The NPV is greatly affected by the discount rate. Thus, identifying the proper discount rate-often termed, the project "hurdle rate"-is critical to making an appropriate decision. The hurdle rate is the minimum acceptable return on an investment—i.e. the project appropriate discount rate. The hurdle rate should reflect the riskiness of the investment, typically measured by volatility of cash flows, and must take into account the financing mix. Managers use models such as the CAPM or the APT to estimate a discount rate appropriate for a particular project, and use the weighted average cost of capital (*WACC*) to reflect the financing mix selected. (A common error in choosing a discount rate for a project is to apply a WACC that applies to the entire firm. Such an approach may not be appropriate where the risk of a particular project differs markedly from that of the firm's existing portfolio of assets.)

In conjunction with NPV, there are several other measures used as (secondary) selection criteria in corporate finance. These are visible from the DCF and include discounted payback period, IRR, Modified IRR, equivalent annuity, capital efficiency, and ROI.

Valuing Flexibility

In many cases, for example R&D projects, a project may open (or close) paths of action to the company, but this reality will not typically be captured in a strict NPV approach. Management will therefore (sometimes) employ tools which place an explicit value on these options. So, whereas in a DCF valuation the most likely or average or scenario specific cash flows are discounted, here the "flexibile and staged nature" of the investment is modelled, and hence "all" potential payoffs are considered. The difference between the two valuations is the "value of flexibility" inherent in the project.

The two most common tools are Decision Tree Analysis (DTA) and Real options analysis (ROA); they may often be used interchangeably:

- DTA values flexibility by incorporating *possible events* (or states) and consequent *management decisions*. (For example, a company would build a factory given that demand for its product exceeded a certain level during the pilot-phase, and outsource production otherwise. In turn, given further demand, it would similarly expand the factory, and maintain it otherwise. In a DCF model, by contrast, there is no "branching"-each scenario must be modelled separately.) In the decision tree, each management decision in response to an "event" generates a "branch" or "path" which the company could follow; the probabilities of each event are determined or specified by management. Once the tree is constructed: (1) "all" possible events and their resultant paths are visible to management; (2) given this "knowledge" of the events that could follow, management chooses the actions corresponding to the highest value path probability weighted; (3) then, assuming rational decision making, this path is taken as representative of project value.
- ROA is usually used when the value of a project is *contingent* on the *value* of some other asset or underlying variable. (For example, the viability of a mining project is contingent on the price of gold; if the price is too low, management will abandon the mining rights, if sufficiently high, management will develop the ore body. Again, a DCF valuation would capture only one of these outcomes.) Here: (1) using financial option theory as a framework, the decision to be taken is identified as corresponding to either a call option or a put option; (2) an appropriate valuation technique is then employed-usually a variant on the Binomial options model or a bespoke simulation model, while Black Scholes type formulae are used less often-see Contingent claim valuation. The "true" value of the project is then the NPV of the "most likely" scenario plus the option value.

Quantifying Uncertainty

Given the uncertainty inherent in project forecasting and

valuation, analysts will wish to assess the *sensitivity* of project NPV to the various inputs (i.e. assumptions) to the DCF model. In a typical sensitivity analysis the analyst will vary one key factor while holding all other inputs constant, *ceteris paribus*. The sensitivity of NPV to a change in that factor is then observed, and is calculated as a "slope": NPV/factor.

For example, the analyst will determine NPV at various growth rates in annual revenue as specified (usually at set increments, e.g.-10%,-5%, 0%, 5%....), and then determine the sensitivity using this formula. Often, several variables may be of interest, and their various combinations produce a "value-surface" (or even a "value-space"), where NPV is then a function of several variables.

Using a related technique, analysts also run scenario based forecasts of NPV. Here, a scenario comprises a particular outcome for economy-wide, "global" factors (demand for the product, exchange rates, commodity prices, etc...) *as well as* for company-specific factors (unit costs, etc...). As an example, the analyst may specify specific growth scenarios (e.g. 5% for "Worst Case", 10% for "Likely Case" and 25% for "Best Case"), where all key inputs are adjusted so as to be consistent with the growth assumptions, and calculate the NPV for each. Note that for scenario based analysis, the various combinations of inputs must be *internally consistent*, whereas for the sensitivity approach these need not be so. An application of this methodology is to determine an "unbiased" NPV, where management determines a (subjective) probability for each scenario – the NPV for the project is then the probability-weighted average of the various scenarios.

A further advancement is to construct stochastic or probabilistic financial models – as opposed to the traditional static and deterministic models as above. For this purpose, the most common method is to use Monte Carlo simulation to analyse the project's NPV. This method was introduced to finance by David B. Hertz in 1964, although has only recently become common: today analysts are even able to run simulations in spreadsheet based DCF models, typically using an add-in, such as Crystal Ball. Using simulation, the cash flow components that are (heavily) impacted by uncertainty are simulated, mathematically reflecting their "random characteristics". Here, in contrast to the scenario approach above, the simulation produces several *thousand* random but possible outcomes, or "trials"; see Monte Carlo Simulation versus "What If" Scenarios. The output is then a histogram of project NPV, and the average NPV of the potential investment – as well as its volatility and other sensitivities – is then observed. This histogram provides information not visible from the static DCF: for example, it allows for an estimate of the probability that a project has a net present value greater than zero (or any other value).

Continuing the above example: instead of assigning three discrete values to revenue growth, and to the other relevant variables, the analyst would assign an appropriate probability distribution to each variable (commonly triangular or beta), and, where possible, specify the observed or supposed correlation between the variables. These distributions would then be "sampled" repeatedly-incorporating this correlation-so as to generate several thousand scenarios, with corresponding valuations, which are then used to generate the NPV histogram. The resultant statistics (average NPV and standard deviation of NPV) will be a more accurate mirror of the project's "randomness" than the variance observed under the scenario based approach.

The Financing Decision

Achieving the goals of corporate finance requires that any corporate investment be financed appropriately. As above, since both hurdle rate and cash flows (and hence the riskiness of the firm) will be affected, the financing mix can impact the valuation. Management must therefore identify the "optimal mix" of financing—the capital structure that results in maximum value.

The sources of financing will, generically, comprise some combination of debt and equity financing. Financing a project through debt results in a liability or obligation that must be serviced, thus entailing cash flow implications independent of the project's degree of success. Equity financing is less risky with respect to cash flow commitments, but results in a dilution of ownership, control and earnings. The *cost of equity* is also typically higher than the *cost of debt*, and so equity financing may result in an increased hurdle rate which may offset any reduction in cash flow risk.

Management must also attempt to match the financing mix to the asset being financed as closely as possible, in terms of both timing and cash flows.

One of the main theories of how firms make their financing decisions is the Pecking Order Theory, which suggests that firms avoid external financing while they have internal financing available and avoid new equity financing while they can engage in new debt financing at reasonably low interest rates. Another major theory is the Trade-Off Theory in which firms are assumed to trade-off the tax benefits of debt with the bankruptcy costs of debt when making their decisions. An emerging area in finance theory is right-financing whereby investment banks and corporations can enhance investment return and company value over time by determining the right investment objectives, policy framework, institutional structure, source of financing (debt or equity) and expenditure framework within a given economy and under given market conditions. One last theory about this decision is the Market timing hypothesis which states that firms look for the cheaper type of financing regardless of their current levels of internal resources, debt and equity.

The Dividend Decision

Whether to issue dividends, and what amount, is calculated mainly on the basis of the company's unappropriated profit and its earning prospects for the coming year. If there are no NPV positive opportunities, i.e. projects where returns exceed the hurdle rate, then management must return excess cash to investors. These *free cash flows* comprise cash remaining after all business expenses have been met.

This is the general case, however there are exceptions. For example, investors in a "Growth stock", expect that the company will, almost by definition, retain earnings so as to fund growth internally. In other cases, even though an opportunity is currently NPV negative, management may consider "investment flexibility"/ potential payoffs and decide to retain cash flows.

Management must also decide on the form of the dividend distribution, generally as cash dividends or via a share buyback. Various factors may be taken into consideration: where shareholders must pay tax on dividends, firms may elect to retain earnings or to perform a stock buyback, in both cases increasing the value of shares outstanding. Alternatively, some companies will pay "dividends" from stock rather than in cash; see Corporate action. Today, it is generally accepted that dividend policy is value neutral.

Working Capital Management

Decisions relating to working capital and short term financing are referred to as *working capital management*. These involve managing the relationship between a firm's short-term assets and its short-term liabilities. As above, the goal of Corporate Finance is the maximization of firm value. In the context of long term, capital investment decisions, firm value is enhanced through appropriately selecting and funding NPV positive investments. These investments, in turn, have implications in terms of cash flow and cost of capital. The goal of Working capital management is therefore to ensure that the firm is able to operate, and that it has sufficient cash flow to service long term debt, and to satisfy both maturing short-term debt and upcoming operational expenses. In so doing, firm value is enhanced when, and if, the return on capital exceeds the cost of capital.

Decision Criteria

Working capital is the amount of capital which is readily available to an organization. That is, working capital is the difference between resources in cash or readily convertible into cash (Current Assets), and cash requirements (Current Liabilities). As a result, the decisions relating to working capital are always current, i.e. short term, decisions.

In addition to time horizon, working capital decisions differ from capital investment decisions in terms of discounting and profitability considerations; they are also "reversible" to some extent. (Considerations as to Risk appetite and return targets remain identical, although some constraints-such as those imposed by loan covenants-may be more relevant here).

Working capital management decisions are therefore not taken on the same basis as long term decisions, and working capital management applies different criteria in decision making: the main considerations are (1) cash flow/liquidity and (2) profitability/ return on capital (of which cash flow is probably the more important).

- The most widely used measure of cash flow is the net operating cycle, or cash conversion cycle. This represents the time difference between cash payment for raw materials and cash collection for sales. The cash conversion cycle indicates the firm's ability to convert its resources into cash. Because this number effectively corresponds to the time that the firm's cash is tied up in operations and unavailable for other activities, management generally aims at a low net count. (Another measure is gross operating cycle which is the same as net operating cycle except that it does not take into account the creditors deferral period.)
- In this context, the most useful measure of profitability is Return on capital (ROC). The result is shown as a percentage, determined by dividing relevant income for the 12 months by capital employed; Return on equity (ROE) shows this result for the firm's shareholders. As above, firm value is enhanced when, and if, the return on capital, exceeds the cost of capital. ROC measures are therefore useful as a management tool, in that they link short-term policy with long-term decision making.

Management of Working Capital

Guided by the above criteria, management will use a combination of policies and techniques for the management of working capital. These policies aim at managing the *current assets* (generally cash and cash equivalents, inventories and debtors) and the short term financing, such that cash flows and returns are acceptable.

- Cash management. Identify the cash balance which allows for the business to meet day to day expenses, but reduces cash holding costs.
- Inventory management. Identify the level of inventory which allows for uninterrupted production but reduces

the investment in raw materials-and minimizes reordering costs-and hence increases cash flow; see Supply chain management; Just In Time (JIT); Economic order quantity (EOQ); Economic production quantity (EPQ).

- Debtors management. Identify the appropriate credit policy, i.e. credit terms which will attract customers, such that any impact on cash flows and the cash conversion cycle will be offset by increased revenue and hence Return on Capital (or *vice versa*).
- Short term financing. Identify the appropriate source of financing, given the cash conversion cycle: the inventory is ideally financed by credit granted by the supplier; however, it may be necessary to utilize a bank loan (or overdraft), or to "convert debtors to cash" through "factoring".

Financial Risk Management

Risk management is the process of measuring risk and then developing and implementing strategies to manage that risk. Financial risk management focuses on risks that can be managed ("hedged") using traded financial instruments (typically changes in commodity prices, interest rates, foreign exchange rates and stock prices). Financial risk management will also play an important role in cash management.

This area is related to corporate finance in two ways. Firstly, firm exposure to business risk is a direct result of previous Investment and Financing decisions. Secondly, both disciplines share the goal of enhancing, or preserving, firm value. All large corporations have risk management teams, and small firms practice informal, if not formal, risk management.

Derivatives are the instruments most commonly used in financial risk management. Because unique derivative contracts tend to be costly to create and monitor, the most cost-effective financial risk management methods usually involve derivatives that trade on well-established financial markets. These standard derivative instruments include options, futures contracts, forward contracts, and swaps.

Relationship with other Areas in Finance

Investment Banking

Use of the term "corporate finance" varies considerably across the world. In the United States it is used, as above, to describe activities, decisions and techniques that deal with many aspects of a company's finances and capital. In the United Kingdom and Commonwealth countries, the terms "corporate finance" and "corporate financier" tend to be associated with investment banking-i.e. with transactions in which capital is raised for the corporation.

Personal and Public Finance

Corporate finance utilizes tools from almost all areas of finance. Some of the tools developed by and for corporations have broad application to entities other than corporations, for example, to partnerships, sole proprietorships, not-for-profit organizations, governments, mutual funds, and personal wealth management. But in other cases their application is very limited outside of the corporate finance arena. Because corporations deal in quantities of money much greater than individuals, the analysis has developed into a discipline of its own. It can be differentiated from personal finance and public finance.

Financial Plan

In general usage, a financial plan can be a budget, a plan for spending and saving future income. This plan allocates future income to various types of expenses, such as rent or utilities, and also reserves some income for short-term and long-term savings. A financial plan can also be an investment plan, which allocates savings to various assets or projects expected to produce future income, such as a new business or product line, shares in an existing business, or real estate.

In business, a financial plan can refer to the three primary financial statements (balance sheet, income statement, and cash flow statement) created within a business plan. Financial forecast or financial plan can also refer to an annual projection of income and expenses for a company, division or department. A financial plan can also be an estimation of cash needs and a decision on how to raise the cash, such as through borrowing or issuing additional shares in a company.

While a financial plan refers to estimating future income, expenses and assets, a financing plan or finance plan usually refers to the means by which cash will be acquired to cover future expenses, for instance through earning, borrowing or using saved cash.

Accountancy

Accountancy is the art of communicating financial information about a business entity to users such as shareholders and managers. The communication is generally in the form of financial statements that show in money terms the economic resources under the control of management; the art lies in selecting the information that is relevant to the user and is reliable. Accountancy is a branch of mathematical science that is useful in discovering the causes of success and failure in business. The principles of accountancy are applied to business entities in three divisions of practical art, named accounting, bookkeeping, and auditing.

Accounting is defined by the AICPA as "The art of recording, classifying, and summarizing in a significant manner and in terms of money, transactions and events which are, in part at least, of financial character, and interpreting the results thereof."

Accounting is thousands of years old; the earliest accounting records, which date back more than 7,000 years, were found in the Middle East. The people of that time relied on primitive accounting methods to record the growth of crops and herds. Accounting evolved, improving over the years and advancing as business advanced.

Early accounts served mainly to assist the memory of the businessperson and the audience for the account was the proprietor or record keeper alone. Cruder forms of accounting were inadequate for the problems created by a business entity involving multiple investors, so double-entry bookkeeping first emerged in northern Italy in the 14th century, where trading ventures began to require more capital than a single individual was able to invest.

The development of joint stock companies created wider audiences for accounts, as investors without firsthand knowledge of their operations relied on accounts to provide the requisite information. This development resulted in a split of accounting systems for internal (i.e. management accounting) and external (i.e. financial accounting) purposes, and subsequently also in accounting and disclosure regulations and a growing need for independent attestation of external accounts by auditors.

Today, accounting is called "the language of business" because it is the vehicle for reporting financial information about a business entity to many different groups of people. Accounting that concentrates on reporting to people inside the business entity is called management accounting and is used to provide information to employees, managers, owner-managers and auditors. Management accounting is concerned primarily with providing a basis for making management or operating decisions. Accounting that provides information to people outside the business entity is called financial accounting and provides information to present and potential shareholders, creditors such as banks or vendors, financial analysts, economists, and government agencies. Because these users have different needs, the presentation of financial accounts is very structured and subject to many more rules than management accounting. The body of rules that governs financial accounting is called Generally Accepted Accounting Principles, or GAAP.

Etymology

The word "Accountant" is derived from the French word *Computer,* which took its origin from the Latin word *Computare.* The word was formerly written in English as "Accomptant", but in process of time the word, which was always pronounced by dropping the "p", became gradually changed both in pronunciation and in orthography to its present form.

History

Token Accounting in Ancient Mesopotamia

The earliest accounting records were found amongst the ruins of ancient Babylon, Assyria and Sumeria, which date back more than 7,000 years. The people of that time relied on primitive accounting methods to record the growth of crops and herds. Because there is a natural season to farming and herding, it is easy to count and determine if a surplus had been gained after the crops had been harvested or the young animals weaned.

During the period 8000–3700 BCE, the Fertile Crescent witnessed the spread of small settlements supported by agricultural surplus. Tokens, shaped into simple geometric forms such as cones or spheres, were used for stewardship purposes in relation to identifying and securing this surplus, and are examples of accounts that referred to lists of personal property. Some of them bore markings in the form of incised lines and impressed dots. Neolithic community leaders collected the surplus at regular intervals in the form of a share of the farmers' flocks and harvests. In turn, the accumulated communal goods were redistributed to those who could not support themselves, but the greatest part was earmarked for the performance of religious rituals and festivals. In 7000 BCE, there were only some 10 token shapes because the system exclusively recorded agricultural goods, each representing one of the farm products levied at the time, such as grain, oil and domesticated animals. The number of token shapes increased to about 350 around 3500 BCE, when urban workshops started contributing to the redistribution economy. Some of the new tokens stood for raw materials such as wool and metal and others for finished products among which textiles, garments, jewelry, bread, beer and honey.

The invention of a form of bookkeeping using clay tokens represented a huge cognitive leap for mankind. The cognitive significance of the token system was to foster the manipulation of data. Compared to oral information passed on from one individual to the other, tokens were extra-somatic, that is outside the human mind. As a result, the Neolithic accountants were no longer the passive recipients of someone else's knowledge, but they took an active part in encoding and decoding data. The token system substituted miniature counters for the real goods, which eliminated their bulk and weight and allowed dealing with them in abstraction by patterning, the presentation of data in particular configurations. As a result, heavy baskets of grains and animals difficult to control could be easily counted and recounted. The accountants could add, subtract, multiply and divide by manually moving and removing counters.

The Mesopotamian civilization emerged during the period 3700–2900 BCE amid the development of technological innovations such as the plough, sailing boats and copper metal working. Clay tablets with pictographic characters appeared in this period to record commercial transactions performed by the temples. Clay receptacles known as *bullae* (Latin: 'Bubble'), were used in Elamite city of Susa which contained tokens. These receptacles were spherical in shape and acted as envelopes, on which the seal of the individuals taking part in a transaction were engraved. The symbols of the tokens they contained were represented graphically on their surface, and the recipient of the goods could check whether they matched with the amount and characteristics expressed on the bulla once they had received and inspected them. The fact that the content of *bulla* was marked on its surface produced a simple way of checking without destroying the receptacle, which constituted in itself an exercise in writing that, despite being born spontaneously as a support for the existing system for controlling merchant goods, ultimately became the definitive practice for non-oral communication. Eventually, *bullae* were replaced by clay tablets, which used symbols to represent the tokens. During the Sumerian period, token envelop accounting was replaced by flat clay tablets impressed by tokens that merely transferred symbols. Such documents were kept by scribes, who were carefully trained to acquire the necessary literary and arithmetic skills and were held responsible for documenting financial transactions. Such records preceded the earliest found examples of cuneiform writing in the form of abstract signs incised in clay tablets, which were written in Sumerian by 2900 BCE in Jemdet Nasr. Therefore "token envelop accounting" not only preceded the written word but constituted the major impetus in the creation of writing and abstract counting.

Accounting in the Roman Empire

The *Res Gestae Divi Augusti* (Latin: "The Deeds of the Divine Augustus") is a remarkable account to the Roman people of the

Emperor Augustus' stewardship. It listed and quantified his public expenditure, which encompassed distributions to the people, grants of land or money to army veterans, subsidies to the *aerarium* (treasury), building of temples, religious offerings, and expenditures on theatrical shows and gladiatorial games. It was not an account of state revenue and expenditure, but was designed to demonstrate Augustus' munificence. The significance of the *Res Gestae Divi Augusti* from an accounting perspective lies in the fact that it illustrates that the executive authority had access to detailed financial information, covering a period of some forty years, which was still retrievable after the event. The scope of the accounting information at the emperor's disposal suggests that its purpose encompassed planning and decision-making.

The Roman historians Suetonius and Cassius Dio record that in 23 BC, Augustus prepared a *rationarium* (account) which listed public revenues, the amounts of cash in the *aerarium* (treasury), in the provincial *fisci* (tax officials), and in the hands of the *publicani* (public contractors); and that it included the names of the freedmen and slaves from whom a detailed account could be obtained. The closeness of this information to the executive authority of the emperor is attested by Tacitus' statement that it was written out by Augustus himself.

Records of cash, commodities, and transactions were kept scrupulously by military personnel of the Roman army. An account of small cash sums received over a few days at the fort of Vindolanda cira 110 CE shows that the fort could compute revenues in cash on a daily basis, perhaps from sales of surplus supplies or goods manufactured in the camp, items dispensed to slaves such as *cervesa* (beer) and *clavi caligares* (nails for boots), as well as commodities bought by individual soldiers. The basic needs of the fort were met by a mixture of direct production, purchase and requisition; in one letter, a request for money to buy 5,000 *modii* (measures) of *braces* (a cereal used in brewing) shows that the fort bought provisions for a considerable number of people.

The Heroninos Archive is name given to a huge collection of papyrus documents, mostly letters, but also including a fair number of accounts, which comes from Roman Egypt in 3rd century CE.

The bulk of the documents relate to the running of a large, private estate is named after Heroninos because he was *phrontistes* (Koine Greek: manager) of the estate which had a complex and standarised system of accounting which was followed by all its local farm managers. Each administrator on each sub-division of the estate drew up his own little accounts, for day to day running of the estate, payment of the workforce, production of crops, the sale produce, the use of animals, and general expetidirure on the staff. This information was then summarized as pieces of papyrus scroll into one big yearly account for each particular sub—division of the estate. Entries were arranged by sector, with cash expenses and gains extrapolated from all the different sectors. Accounts of this kind gave the owner the opportunity to take better economic decisions because the information was purposefully selected and arranged.

Simple accounting is mentioned in the Christian Bible (New Testament) in the Book of Matthew, in the Parable of the Talents.

Islamic Accounting & Algebra

In the Holy Qur'an, the word *hesab* (Arabic: account) is used in its generic sense, relating to one's obligation to account to God on all matters pertaining to human endeavour. According to the Holy Qur'an, followers are required to keep records of their indebtedness (Sura 2, ayah 282), thus Islam thus provides general approval and guidelines for the recording and reporting of transactions.

The Islamic law of inheritance (Sura 4, ayah 11) defines exactly how the estate is calculated after death of an individual. The power of testamentary disposition is basically limited to one-third of the net estate (i.e. the assets remaining after the payment of funeral expenses and debts), providing for every member of the family by allotting fixed shares not only to wives and children, but also to father and mothers. The complexity of this law served as an impetus behind the development of algebra (Arabic: *al-jabr*) by Muhammad ibn Musa al-Khwarizmî and other medieval Islamic mathematicians.

The development of mathematics and accounting was intertwined during the Renaissance. Mathematics was in the midst of a period of significant development in the late 15th century. Hindu-Arabic numerals and algebra were introduced to Europe from Arab mathematics at the end of the 10th century by the Benedictine monk Gerbert of Aurillac, but it was only after Leonardo Pisano (also known as Fibonacci) put commercial arithmetic, Hindu-Arabic numerals, and the rules of algebra together in his Liber Abaci in 1202 that Hindu-Arabic numerals became widely used in Italy.

While there is no direct relationship between algebra and bookkeeping, the teaching of the subjects and the books published addressed the same group, namely the children of merchants who were sent to reckoning schools (in Flanders and Germany) or abacus schools (known as *abbaco* in Italy), where they learned the skills useful for trade and commerce. There is probably no need for algebra in performing bookkeeping operations, but for complex bartering operations or the calculation of compound interest, a basic knowledge of arithmetic was mandatory and knowledge of algebra was very useful.

Luca Pacioli and Double-entry Bookkeeping

Bartering was the dominant practice for travelling merchants during the Middle Ages. When medieval Europe moved to a monetary economy in the 13th century, sedentary merchants depended on bookkeeping to oversee multiple simultaneous transactions financed by bank loans. One important breakthrough took place around that time: the introduction of double-entry bookkeeping, which is defined as any bookkeeping system in which there was a debit and credit entry for each transaction, or for which the majority of transactions were intended to be of this form. The historical origin of the use of the words 'debit' and 'credit' in accounting goes back to the days of single-entry bookkeeping in which the chief objective was to keep track of amounts owed by customers (debtors) and amounts owed to creditors. 'Debit,' is Latin for 'he owes' and 'credit' Latin for 'he trusts'.

The earliest extant evidence of full double-entry bookkeeping is the Farolfi ledger of 1299-1300. Giovanno Farolfi & Company were a firm of Florentine merchants whose head office was in

Nîmes who also acted as moneylenders to Archbishop of Arles, their most important customer. The oldest discovered record of a complete double-entry system is the *Messari* (Italian: Treasurer's) accounts of the city of Genoa in 1340. The *Messari* accounts contain debits and credits journalised in a bilateral form, and contains balances carried forward from the preceding year, and therefore enjoy general recognition as a double-entry system.

Luca Pacioli's *"Summa de Arithmetica, Geometria, Proportioni et Proportionalità"* (Italian: "Review of Arithmetic, Geometry, Ratio and Proportion") was first printed and published in Venice in 1494. It included a 27-page treatise on bookkeeping, *"Particularis de Computis et Scripturis"* (Italian: "Details of Calculation and Recording"). It was written primarily for, and sold mainly to, merchants who used the book as a reference text, as a source of pleasure from the mathematical puzzles it contained, and to aid the education of their sons. It represents the first known printed treatise on bookkeeping; and it is widely believed to be the forerunner of modern bookkeeping practice. In *Summa Arithmetica,* Pacioli introduced symbols for plus and minus for the first time in a printed book, symbols that became standard notation in Italian Renaissance mathematics. *Summa Arithmetica* was also the first known book printed in Italy to contain algebra.

Although Luca Pacioli did not invent double-entry bookkeeping,, his 27-page treatise on bookkeeping contained the first known published work on that topic, and is said to have laid the foundation for double-entry bookkeeping as it is practiced today. Even though Pacioli's treatise exhibits almost no originality, it is generally considered as an important work, mainly because of its wide circulation, it was written in vernacular Italian language, and it was a printed book.

According to Pacioli, accounting is an ad hoc ordering system devised by the merchant. Its regular use provides the merchant with continued information about his business, and allows him to evaluate how things are going and to act accordingly. Pacioli recommends the Venetian method of double-entry bookkeeping above all others. Three major books of account are at the direct basis of this system: the *memoriale* (Italian: memorandum), the *giornale* (journal), and the *quaderno* (ledger). The ledger is considered as the central one and is accompanied by an alphabetical index. Pacioli's treatise gave instructions in how to record barter transactions and transactions in a variety of currencies – both being far more commonplace than they are today. It also enabled merchants to audit their own books and to ensure that the entries in the accounting records made by their bookkeepers complied with the method he described. Without such a system, all merchants who did not maintain their own records were at greater risk of theft by their employees and agents: it is not by accident that the first and last items described in his treatise concern maintenance of an accurate inventory. The nature of double-entry can be grasped by recognizing that this system of bookkeeping did not simply record the things merchants traded so that they could keep track of assets or calculate profits and losses; instead as a system of writing, double-entry produced effects that exceeded transcription and calculation. One of its social effects was to proclaim the honesty of merchants as a group; one of its epistemological effects was to make its formal precision based on a rule bound system of arithmetic seem to guarantee the accuracy of the details it recorded. Even though the information recorded in the books of account was not necessarily accurate, the combination of the double entry system's precision and the normalizing effect that precision tended to create the impression that books of account were not only precise, but accurate as well. Instead of gaining prestige from numbers, double entry bookkeeping helped confer cultural authority on numbers.

Post-Pacioli

The spread of the Italian accounting rules over the rest of Europe and thence further afield, was the result of treatises, some of them strongly based on Pacioli's work, describing and explaining the system and its practice. The *"Quaderno doppio"* (trans. Double-entry Ledger, Venice, 1534) of Domenico Manzoni da Oderzo was one of the first reproductions of Pacioli's *"Particularis de Computis et Scripturis"*. This work, important because of elaborate examples, was very popular and widespread among merchants: it enjoyed no less than seven editions between 1534 and 1574. Other books that are directly or indirectly based on Pacioli's work are Hugh Oldcastle's *"A Profitable Treatyce called the Instrument or Boke to learne to knowe the good order of the kepyng of the famous reconynge called in Latyn, Dare and Habere, and in Englyshe, Debitor and Creditor"* (London, 1543), a translation of Pacioli's treatise, and Wolfgang Schweicker's *"Zwifach Buchhalten"* (trans. Double-entry bookkeeping, Neurenberg, 1549), a translation of the *"Quaderno doppio"*.

It was the Dutch mathematician Simon Stevin who persuaded merchants to make it a rule to summarize accounts at the end of every year in a chapter entitled *Coopmansbouckhouding op de Italiaensche wyse* (Dutch: "Commercial Book-keeping in the Italian Way") of his *Wisconstigheg hedachtenissen* (Dutch: "Mathematical memoirs", Leiden, 1605–08). Although the balance sheet he required every enterprise to prepare every year was based on entries of the ledger, it was prepared separately from the major books of account. The oldest semi-public balance sheet recorded was that of the East India Company dated 30 April 1671, which was submitted to the company's General Meeting on in 30 August 1671. The publication and audit of the balance sheet was still a rarity in England until the passing of the Bank Charter Act 1844.

In 1863, the Dowlais Iron Company had receovered from a business slump, but had no cash to invest for a new blast furnace, despite having made a profit. To explain why there were no funds to invest, the manager made a new financial statement that was called a *comparison balance sheet,* which showed that the company was holding too much inventory. This new financial statement was the genesis of Cash Flow Statement that is used today.

Between the publication of Pacioli's *"Particularis de Computis et Scripturis"* and the 19th century, there were few other changes in accounting theory. There was a general theoretical consensus that the double-entry method was superior because it could solve so many accounting problems simultaneously, but despite this consensus, accounting practices were remarkably varied, and merchants in the 16th and 17th centuries seldom maintained the high standards of the double-entry method. The application of double entry bookkeeping varied across countries, industries, and individual firms, depending in part on its audience. This audience shifted in general from sole proprietorship alone to a larger more dispersed group of partnership, coinvestors, shareholders, and even eventually the state, as capitalism became more sophisticated.

In the Ottoman Empire, which at its peak ruled over Anatolia, Middle East, North Africa, the Balkans and parts of Eastern Europe, the *merdiban* (Persian: ladder or stairs) accounting system that had been adopted from the Ilkhanate in the 14th century was used for 500 years until the end of the 19th century. Both the Ilkhanians and the Ottomans used *siyakat* script (from the Arabic *siyak,* to lead or herd), which was stenographic writing style of Arabic used only in official documents which prevented ordinary people from reading important state correspondence. The title for each entry is given by extending the last letter of the first word in a straight line, so that the lines between successive entries would be laid out in the style of steps of a ladder. Permission to replace the *merdiban* accounting system with double-entry accounting was given by Sultan Abdülhamid II to the Ministry of Finance in 1880.

Accounting Scandals

The year 2001 witnessed a series of financial information frauds involving Enron Corporation, auditing firm Arthur Andersen, the telecommunications company WorldCom, Qwest and Sunbeam, among other well-known corporations. These problems highlighted the need to review the effectiveness of accounting standards, auditing regulations and corporate governance principles. In some cases, management manipulated the figures shown in financial reports to indicate a better economic performance. In others, tax and regulatory incentives encouraged over-leveraging of companies and decisions to bear extraordinary and unjustified risk.

The Enron scandal deeply influenced the development of new regulations to improve the reliability of financial reporting, and increased public awareness about the importance of having accounting standards that show the financial reality of companies and the objectivity and independence of auditing firms. In addition to being the largest bankruptcy reorganization in American history, the Enron scandal undoubtedly is the biggest audit failure. The scandal caused the dissolution of Arthur Andersen, which at the time was one of the five largest accounting firms in the world. It involved a financial scandal of Enron Corporation and their auditors

Arthur Andersen, which was revealed in late 2001. After a series of revelations involving irregular accounting procedures conducted throughout the 1990s.

One consequence of these events was the passage of Sarbanes-Oxley Act in 2002, as a result of the first admissions of fraudulent behaviour made by Enron. The act significantly raises criminal penalties for securities fraud, for destroying, altering or fabricating records in federal investigations or any scheme or attempt to defraud shareholders.

Accountant

An accountant is a practitioner of accountancy (called accounting in the United States), which is the measurement, disclosure or provision of assurance about financial information that helps managers, investors, tax authorities and other decision makers make resource allocation decisions.

The word "accountant" is derived from the French word *Compter* which took its origin from the Latin word *Computare*. The word was written in Middle English as *Accomptant*, but in process of time the word, which was always pronounced by dropping the "p", became gradually changed both in pronunciation and in orthography to its present form. The Big Four are the largest employers of accountants worldwide.

Commonwealth of Nations

In the Commonwealth of Nations, which includes the United Kingdom, Canada, Australia, New Zealand and several other states, the equivalents of Certified Public Accountant (CPA) include Chartered Certified Accountant (ACCA), Chartered Accountant (CA or ACA), Chartered Management Accountant, International Accountant (AAIA), Certified Public Accountant (CPA-Ireland and CPA-Hong Kong), Certified Management Accountant (CMA-Canada), Certified General Accountant (CGA-Canada), Certified Practicing Accountant (CPA-Australia) and members of the NIA (Australia), Certified Public Practicing Accountant (CPPA) of the New Zealand Association of Certified Public Accountants (NZACPA) the operating name of New Zealand Association of Accountants Inc (NZAA).

United Kingdom

- A Chartered Certified Accountant must be a member of the Association of Chartered Certified Accountants (designatory letters ACCA or FCCA).
- A Chartered Accountant must be a member of one of the following:
  - the Institute of Chartered Accountants in England & Wales (ICAEW) (designatory letters ACA or FCA)
  - the Institute of Chartered Accountants of Scotland (ICAS) (designatory letters CA)
  - the Institute of Chartered Accountants in Ireland (ICAI)
  - a recognised equivalent body from another Commonwealth country (designatory letters being CA (name of country) e.g. CA (Canada)).
- A Chartered Management Accountant must be a member of the Chartered Institute of Management Accountants (designatory letters ACMA or FCMA).
- A Chartered Public Finance Accountant must be a member of the Chartered Institute of Public Finance and Accountancy (designatory letters CPFA).
- An International Accountant must be a member of the Association of International Accountants (designatory letters AIAA or FAIA).
- An Incorporated Financial Accountant must be a member of the Institute of Financial Accountants (designatory letters AFA or FFA).
- A Certified Public Accountant must be a member of the Association of Certified Public Accountants (designatory letters AICPA or FCPA).

Except Association of Certified Public Accountants, each of above bodies admits members only after passing examinations and undergoing a period of relevant work experience. Once admitted members are expected to comply with ethical guidelines and gain appropriate professional experience. Chartered, Chartered Certified, Chartered Public Finance, and International Accountant engaging in practice (i.e. selling services to the public rather than acting as an employee) must gain a "practicing certificate" by meeting further requirements such as purchasing adequate insurance and undergoing inspections.

ICAEW, ICAS, ICAI, ACCA, AIA and CIPFA as six statutory RQB Qualification Bodies in UK, the member of them may also become *Registered Auditors* in accordance with the Companies Act, providing they can demonstrate the necessary professional ability in that area and submit to regular inspection. It is illegal for any individual or firm that is not a Registered Auditor to perform a company audit.

Further restrictions apply to accountants who carry out insolvency work.

In addition to the bodies above, the Association of Accounting Technicians and Association of Certified Accounting Technicians offers its members training and support in accountancy skills.

Canada

In Canada, there are three recognized accounting bodies: the Canadian Institute of Chartered Accountants (CA) and the provincial and territorial CA Institutes, the Certified General Accountants Association of Canada (CGA), and the Society of Management Accountants of Canada, also known as the Certified Management Accountants (CMA). CA and CGA were created by Acts of Parliament in 1902 and 1913 respectively and CMA was established in 1920.

The CA program focuses on public accounting and candidates must obtain auditing experience from public accounting firms; the CGA program takes a general approach allowing candidates to focus in their own financial career choices; the CMA program focuses in management accounting, but also provides a general approach to financial accounting and tax. The CA and CMA programs require a candidate to obtain a degree as a program entry requirement. The CGA program requires a degree as an exit requirement prior to certification.

Auditing and Public Accounting are regulated by the provinces. Historically, only CAs can perform audits in Ontario. In 2004, the provincial government of Ontario passed a new Public Accounting Act that would allow qualified CGAs and CMAs to perform audits, conditional on their organizations being able to demonstrate that their qualification and regulatory programs are equivalent in rigour to that of the CA program. As of March 2006, this process of evaluation had not yet begun. On November 20, 2009, Quebec passed regulations granting qualified CAs, CMAs and CGAs statutory auditing rights. In British Columbia and Prince Edward Island, CAs and CGAs have equal status regarding public accounting and auditing; In the rest of Canada, CAs, CMAs, and CGAs are considered equivalents pursuant to provincial and territorial legislation.

As of year 2006, the Chartered Certified Accountant (ACCA or FCCA) is also recognized by Canadian government as an eligible qualification to audit federal government institutions in Canada. Furthermore, The Canadian branch of ACCA is pursuing recognition for statutory audit purposes in the province of Ontario under the province's Public Accounting Act of 2004.

Australia

In Australia there are four main local professional accountancy bodies.

- Certified Practicing Accountants (CPA) are members of CPA Australia.
- Professional National Accountants (PNA) and Member of National Institute of Accountants (MNIA) are members of National Institute of Accountants Australia.
- Chartered Accountants are members of the Institute of Chartered Accountants in Australia.

However, the Chartered Certified Accountant (ACCA or FCCA) qualification is also recognized as a prescribed body for insolvency purposes under the Corporation Act 2001, section 1282 and for audit purposes by ASIC under Practice Statement 180 Auditor recognition in Australia.

Additionally the Institute of Certified Management Accountants (ICMA) awards the CMA designation, and is specialized in the area of Management Accounting. Description:

are excerpt in finance, taxation, and business leadership And work throughout the world in industry Education: The education is Skill based and they need to complete 19 courses which are consisted of 2 business cases

New Zealand

In New Zealand, there are two local accountancy bodies the New Zealand Institute of Chartered Accountants (NZICA) and the New Zealand Association of Certified Public Accountants (NZACPA) the operating name of New Zealand Association of Accountants Inc (NZAA). To audit public companies an individual must be a member of either the NZICA or an otherwise gazetted body. Chartered Certified Accountant (Association of Chartered Certified Accountants or FCCA) qualification has also been gazetted under the relevant act (Under Section 199 of the Companies Act 1993: Qualifications of Auditors). An ACCA member can practice as long as they hold an ACCA public practice certificate (with audit qualification) in their country of origin.

Sri Lanka

In Sri Lanka, a Chartered Accountant must be a member of the Institute of Chartered Accountants of Sri Lanka (designatory letters ACA or FCA), therefore it is the sole local accountancy body. To audit public companies an individual must be a member of the ICASL.

United States

In the United States, legally practicing accountants are Certified Public Accountants (CPAs), and other non-statutory accountants are Certified Internal Auditors (CIAs), Certified Management Accountants (CMAs) and Accredited Business Accountants (ABAs). The difference between these certifications is primarily the legal status and the types of services provided, although individuals may earn more than one certification. Additionally, much accounting work are performed by uncertified individuals, who may be working under the supervision of a certified accountant.

A CPA is licensed by the state of their residence to provide auditing services to the public, although most CPA firms also offer accounting, tax, litigation support, and other financial advisory services. The requirements for receiving the CPA license varies from state to state, although the passage of the Uniform Certified Public Accountant examination is required by all states. This examination is designed and graded by the American Institute of Certified Public Accountants.

A CIA is granted a certificate from the Institute of Internal Auditors (IIA), provided that the candidate passed a rigorous examination of four parts. A CIA mostly provides their services directly to their employer rather than the public.

A CMA is granted a certificate from the Institute of Management Accountants (IMA), provided that the candidate passed a rigorous examination of four parts and meet the practical experience requirement from the IMA. A CMA mostly provides their services directly to their employers rather than the public. A CMA can also provide his services to the public, but to an extent much lesser than that of a CPA.

An ABA is granted accreditation from the Accreditation Council for Accountancy and Taxation (ACAT), provided that the candidate passed the eight-hour Comprehensive Examination for Accreditation in Accounting which tests proficiency in financial accounting, reporting, statement preparation, taxation, business consulting services, business law, and ethics. An ABA specializes in the needs of small-to-mid-size businesses and in financial services to individuals and families. In states where use of the word "accountant" is not permitted by non state licensed individuals, the practitioner may use Accredited Business Adviser.

The United States Department of Labour's Bureau of Labour Statistics estimates that there are about one million persons employed as accountants and auditors in the U.S.

U.S. tax law grants accountants a limited form of accountant-client privilege.

Earnings and Wages

Accountants Median Salary per Industry

- Accounting, tax preparation, bookkeeping, and payroll services $57,020

- Management of companies and enterprises $55,560
- Local government $50,120
- Depository credit intermediation $49,380
- State government $47,200.

Hong Kong

In Hong Kong, the accountancy industry is regulated by the HKICPA under the Professional Accountants Ordinance. The Auditing industry for limited companies is regulated under the Companies Ordinance, and other Ordinances such as the Securities and Futures Ordinance, the Listing Rules, etc.

Removal of requirement for a qualified accountant in the Listing Rules of Hong Kong

In November 2008, the Stock Exchange of Hong Kong Limited has removed the requirement for a qualified accountant from the Listing Rules but expanded the Code Provisions in the Code on Corporate Governance Practices regarding internal controls to make specific references to the responsibility of the directors to conduct an annual review of the adequacy of staffing of the financial reporting function and the oversight role of the audit committee.

Austria

In Austria the accountancy profession is regulated by the Bilanzbuchhaltungsgesetz 2006 (BibuG-Management Accountancy Law).

Portugal

In Portugal, to be a qualified accountant or auditor, having an academic degree is obligatory, and the certification is exclusively awarded by the *Ordem dos Revisores Oficiais de Contas* (OROC), a professional organization. In general, accountants or auditors accredited by the *Ordem dos Revisores Oficiais de Contas* are individuals with university graduation diplomas in business management, economics, mathematics and even law, who after further studies, applied for an exam at the *Ordem dos Revisores Oficiais de Contas* and received the certification to be a ROC (*Revisor Oficial de Contas*), the highest professional qualification in the field of accountancy. Any citizen having a polytechnic degree as accounting technician is also entitled to apply for the exam and certification at the OROC.

Bookkeeping

Bookkeeping is the recording of financial transactions. Transactions include sales, purchases, income, and payments by an individual or organization. Bookkeeping is usually performed by a bookkeeper. Bookkeeping should not be confused with accounting.

The accounting process is usually performed by an accountant. The accountant creates reports from the recorded financial transactions recorded by the bookkeeper. There are some common methods of bookkeeping such as the Single-entry bookkeeping system and the Double-entry bookkeeping system. But while these systems may be seen as "real" bookkeeping, any process that involves the recording of financial transactions is a bookkeeping process.

A bookkeeper (or book-keeper), also known as an accounting clerk or accounting technician, is a person who records the day-to-day financial transactions of an organization. A bookkeeper is usually responsible for writing the "daybooks." The daybooks consist of purchase, sales, receipts, and payments.

The bookkeeper is responsible for ensuring all transactions are recorded in the correct daybook, suppliers ledger, customer ledger, and general ledger. The bookkeeper brings the books to the trial balance stage. An accountant may prepare the income statement and balance sheet using the trial balance and ledgers prepared by the bookkeeper

Bookkeeping Systems

Two common bookkeeping systems used by businesses and other organizations are the single-entry bookkeeping system and the double-entry bookkeeping system. Single-entry bookkeeping uses only income and expense accounts, recorded primarily in a revenue and expense journal. Single-entry bookkeeping is adequate for many small businesses. Double-entry bookkeeping requires posting (recording) each transaction twice, using debits and credits.

Single-entry System

The primary bookkeeping record in single-entry bookkeeping is the cash book, which is similar to a checking (chequing) account register but allocates the income and expenses to various income and expense accounts. Separate account records are maintained for petty cash, accounts payable and receivable, and other relevant transactions such as inventory and travel expenses. These days, single entry bookkeeping can be done with DIY bookkeeping software to speed up manual calculations.

Daybooks

A daybook is a descriptive and chronological (diary-like) record of day-to-day financial transactions also called a *book of original entry*. The daybook's details must be entered formally into journals to enable posting to ledgers. Daybooks include:

- Sales daybook, for recording all the sales invoices.
- Sales credits daybook, for recording all the sales credit notes.
- Purchases daybook, for recording all the purchase invoices.
- Purchases credits daybook, for recording all the purchase credit notes.
- Cash daybook, usually known as the cash book, for recording all money received as well as money paid out. It may be split into two daybooks: receipts daybook for money received in, and payments daybook for money paid out.

Petty Cash Book

A petty cash book is a record of small value purchases usually controlled by imprest system. Items such as coffee, tea, are listed down in the petty cash book.

Journals

A journal is a formal and chronological record of financial transactions before their values are accounted in general ledger as debits and credits. Journals are recorded in the journal daybook, which is one of the books of first entry. For every debit journal there must an equivalent credit journal. There must be at least two journal entries for every transaction recorded.

Ledgers

A ledger (also known as a book of final entry) is a record of accounts, each recorded individually with its balance. Unlike the journal listing chronologically all financial transactions without balances, the ledger summarizes values of one type of financial transactions per account, which constitute the basis for the balance sheet and income statement. Ledgers include:

- Customer ledger, for financial transactions with a customer (sometimes called a sales ledger).
- Supplier ledger, for financial transactions with a supplier (sometimes called a purchase ledger).
- General (nominal) ledger representing assets, liabilities, income, and expenses.

Chart of Accounts

A chart of accounts is a list of the accounts codes that can be identified with numeric, alphabetical, or alphanumeric codes allowing the account to be located in the general ledger.

Computerized Bookkeeping

Computerized bookkeeping removes many of the paper "books" that are used to record transactions and usually enforces double entry bookkeeping.

Online Bookkeeping

Online bookkeeping, or remote bookkeeping, allows source documents and data to reside in web-based applications which allow remote access for bookkeepers and accountants. All entries made into the online software are recorded and stored in a remote location. The online software can be accessed from any location in the world and permit the bookkeeper or data entry person to work from any location with a suitable data communications link.

Trial Balance

A trial balance is a list of all the nominal ledger (general ledger) accounts contained in the ledger of a business. This list will contain the name of the nominal ledger account and the value of that nominal ledger account.

The value of the nominal ledger will hold either a debit balance value or a credit value balance. The debit balance values will be listed in the debit column of the trial balance and the credit value balance will be listed in the credit column.

The profit and loss statement and balance sheet and other financial reports can then be produced using the ledger accounts listed on the trial balance. All trial balances MUST balance hence the name trial balance.

The name comes from the purpose of a trial balance which is to prove that the value of all the debit value balances equal the total of all the credit value balances.

Trialing, by listing every nominal ledger balance, ensures accurate reporting of the nominal ledgers for use in financial reporting of a businesses performance.

If the total of the debit column does not equal the total value of the credit column then this would show that there is an error in the nominal ledger accounts. This error must be found before a profit and loss statement and balance sheet can be produced. The trial balance is usually prepared by a bookkeeper who has used daybooks to record financial transactions and then post them to the nominal ledgers and personal ledger accounts. The trial balance is a part of the double-entry bookkeeping system and uses the classic 'T' account format for presenting values.

Trial Balance Limitations

A trial balance only checks the sum of debits against the sum of credits. That is why it does not guarantee that there are no errors. The following are the main classes of error that are not detected by the trial balance:

- An error of original entry is when both sides of a transaction include the wrong amount. For example, if a purchase invoice for £21 is entered as £12, this will result in an incorrect debit entry (to purchases), and an incorrect credit entry (to the relevant creditor account), both for £9 less, so the total of both columns will be £9 less, and will thus balance.

- An error of omission is when a transaction is completely omitted from the accounting records. As the debits and credits for the transaction would balance, omitting it would still leave the totals balanced. A variation of this error is omitting one of the ledger account totals from the trial balance.
- An error of reversal is when entries are made to the correct amount, but with debits instead of credits, and vice versa. For example, if a cash sale for £100 is debited to the Sales account, and credited to the Cash account. Such an error will not affect the totals.
- An error of commission is when the entries are made at the correct amount, and the appropriate side (debit or credit), but one or more entries are made to the wrong account of the correct type. For example, if fuel costs are incorrectly debited to the postage account (both expense accounts). This will not affect the totals.
- An error of principle is when the entries are made to the correct amount, and the appropriate side (debit or credit), as with an error of commission, but the *wrong* type of account is used. For example, if fuel costs (an expense account), are debited to stock (an asset account). This will not affect the totals.
- Compensating errors are multiple unrelated errors that would individually lead to an imbalance, but together cancel each other out.
- A Transposition Error is a Computing error caused by switching the position of two adjacent digits. Since the resulting error is always divisible by 9, accountants use this fact to locate the misentered number. For example, a total is off by 72, dividing it by 9 gives 8 which indicates that one of the switched digit is either more, or less, by 8 than the other digit. Hence the error was caused by switching the digits 8 and 0 or 1 and 9. This will also not affect the totals.

General Ledger

The general ledger, sometimes known as the nominal ledger, is the main accounting record of a business which uses double-entry bookkeeping. It will usually include accounts for such items as current assets, fixed assets, liabilities, revenue and expense items, gains and losses. Each General Ledger is divided in two sections. The left hand side lists debit transactions and the right hand side lists credit transactions. This gives a 'T' shape to each individual general ledger account.

A "T" account showing debits on the left and credits on the right.

The general ledger is a collection of the group of accounts that supports the value items shown in the major financial statements. It is built up by posting transactions recorded in the sales daybook, purchases daybook, cash book and general journals daybook.

The general ledger can be supported by one or more subsidiary ledgers that provide details for accounts in the general ledger. For instance, an accounts receivable subsidiary ledger would contain a separate account for each credit customer, tracking that customer's balance separately. This subsidiary ledger would then be totalled and compared with its controlling account (in this case, Accounts Receivable) to ensure accuracy as part of the process of preparing a trial balance.

There are seven basic categories in which all accounts are grouped:

1. Assets
2. Liability
3. Owner's equity
4. Revenue
5. Expense
6. Gains (Profits)
7. Losses.

The balance sheet and the income statement are both derived from the general ledger. Each account in the general ledger consists of one or more pages. The general ledger is where posting to the accounts occurs. Posting is the process of recording amounts as credits,, and amounts as debits, in the pages of the general ledger. Additional columns to the right hold a running activity total (similar to a checkbook).

The listing of the account names is called the chart of accounts. The extraction of account balances is called a trial balance. The purpose of the trial balance is, at a preliminary stage of the financial statement preparation process, to ensure the equality of the total debits and credits.

The general ledger should include the date, description and balance or total amount for each account. It is usually divided into at least seven main categories. These categories generally include assets, liabilities, owner's equity, revenue, expenses, gains and losses.

The main categories of the general ledger may be further subdivided into subledgers to include additional details of such accounts as cash, accounts receivable, accounts payable, etc.

Because each bookkeeping entry debits one account and credits another account in an equal amount, the double-entry bookkeeping system helps ensure that the general ledger is always in balance, thus maintaining the accounting equation:

Assets = Liabilities + (Shareholders or Owners equity).

The accounting equation is the mathematical structure of the balance sheet. General Ledger & Sub Ledger.

Debits and Credits

Debit and credit are formal bookkeeping and accounting terms. They are the most fundamental concepts in accounting, representing the two sides of each individual transaction recorded in any accounting system. A debit transaction indicates an asset or an expense transaction, a credit indicates a transaction that will cause a liability or a gain. A debit transaction can also be used to reduce a credit balance or increase a debit balance. A credit transaction can be used to decrease a debit balance or increase a credit balance.

Debits and credits are a system of notation used in bookkeeping to determine how and where to record any financial transaction. In bookkeeping, instead of using addition '+' and subtraction '-' symbols, a transaction uses the symbol DR (Debit) or CR (Credit). In double-entry bookkeeping debit is used for asset and expense transactions and credit is used for liability, gain and equity transactions.

For bank transactions, money in is treated as a debit transaction and money out is treated as a credit transaction. Traditionally, transactions are recorded in two columns of numbers: debits in the left hand column, credits in the right hand column. Keeping the debits and credits in separate columns allows each to be recorded and totalled independently.

Where the total of the debit value amounts is lower than the total of the credit value amounts a balancing debit value is posted to that nominal ledger account. That nominal ledger account is now "balanced". An account can have either a credit value balance or a debit value balance but not both.

Origin of the Terms Debit and Credit

The term debit comes from Middle French *debet* from Latin *debitum* "that which is owed" (the neuter past participle of *debere* "to owe"). Debit is abbreviated to Di (for debtor). The term credit comes from the Latin *creditum* meaning "that which is entrusted or loaned" from the past participle of *credere* "to trust or entrust". Credit is abbreviated to Ck.

Debit and Credit Principle

Each transaction consists of debits and credits, and for every transaction they must be equal.

For Every Transaction: The Value of Debits = The Value of Credits

The extended accounting equation must also balance: '$A + E = L + OE + R$'

(where A = Assets, E = Expenses, L = Liabilities, OE = Owner's Equity and R = Revenues)

So 'Debit Accounts (A + E) = Credit Accounts (L + R + OE)'

Debits are on the left and increase a debit account and reduce a credit account. Credits are on the right and increase a credit account and decrease a debit account.

Operational Principles

- Debit generally represents any depletion in the resources held by the entity while credit represents increment of the resources held by the entity. Hence, debits to an account are negative/depletions in the accounting entity's resources while credits are positive/increments in the same.

Real Accounts

- In real accounts any increment in assets held by the entity is reflected by increasing the relevant asset account and depletion by crediting the asset account.
- If any asset account is debited then it is on account of increment in the value or acquisition of that liability or owner's equity which decreases the resources held by the entity.

As the total resources held by the entity cannot indigenously increment themselves the depletion has to be matched with a fall in resources within the entity.

Personal Accounts

- In Personal Accounts debiting the personal account of any external entity increases the value of the liabilities receivable from that entity thus augmenting the resources of the accounting entity.
- Similarly crediting the personal account of any external entity reduces the value of monies receivable from that entity thus reducing the resources of the accounting entity.

Nominal Accounts

- In Nominal Accounts the Expense accounts whenever debited are done as the Expense incurred represents the Goods and/or Services acquired for ssumption by the entity and hence are temporary increments in the resources of the consumers.

- In Nominal Accounts the Income accounts are credited as the Income earned represents the Epistolary representation of an entity

Simple Thumb Rules to remember which accounts to credit and which to debit:

Personal accounts: Debit: the receiver; Credit: the giver

Real/Asset Accounts: Debit: what comes in; Credit: what goes out

Nominal/Expense Accounts: Debit: all expenses/losses; Credit: all income/gains

Examples

1. when you pay rent with cash: you increase rent (expense) by debiting, and decrease cash (asset) by credit.
2. when you receive cash for a sale: you increase cash (asset) by debiting, and increase sales (revenue) by credit.
3. when you buy equipment (asset) with cash: You increase equipment (asset) by debiting, and decrease cash (asset) by credit.
4. when you borrow with a cash loan: You increase cash (asset) by debiting, and increase loan (liability) by credit.

	Account	*Debit*	*Credit*
1.	Rent	100	
	Cash		100
2.	Cash	50	
	Sale		50
3.	Equip.	5200	
	Cash		5200
4.	Cash	11000	
	Loan		11000

'T' Accounts

The process of using debits and credits creates a ledger format that resembles the letter 'T'. The term "T" account is commonly used when discussing bookkeeping. A 'T' account showing debits on the left and credits on the right.

Standard Accounting Practice

Standard accounting practices require publicly-traded companies to follow certain accounting rules when presenting financial statements so that the readers of the statements can easily compare different companies.

Private companies are also often required by banks and shareholders, for example, to present information according to their specified rules. Usually, countries practicing civil law system write standards into law and countries with English common law systems have private organizations to set the rules.

Common Accounting Standards

Some commonly used accounting standards include:

- Generally accepted accounting principles (United States)
- Generally accepted accounting principles (United Kingdom)
- Grundsatze ordnungsmiger Buchführung (Germany)
- Chinese Accounting Standards (China)
- International Accounting Standards (international).

Rationale for Uniform Practices

The lack of transparent accounting standards in some nations has been cited as increasing the difficulty of doing business in them. In particular, the Asian financial meltdown in the late 1990s has been partially attributed due to the lack of detailed accounting standards. Giant firms in some Asian countries were able to take advantage of their poorly devised accounting standards to cover up immense debts and losses, which yielded a collective effect that eventually led the whole region into financial crisis.

Limitations

The accounting scandals of the early 21st century, which affected companies such as Worldcom and Enron, have shown the limitations of accounting standards in the United States.

Comparison of Cash Method and Accrual Method of Accounting

Two primary accounting methods, *cash* and *accrual basis,* are used to calculate taxable income for U.S. federal income taxes. According to the Internal Revenue Code, a taxpayer may compute taxable income by:

1. the cash receipts and disbursements method;
2. an accrual method;
3. any other method permitted by the chapter; or
4. any combination of the foregoing methods permitted under regulations prescribed by the Secretary.

As a general rule, a taxpayer must compute taxable income using the same accounting method he uses to compute income in keeping his books. Also, the taxpayer must maintain a consistent method of accounting from year to year. Should he change from the cash basis to the accrual basis (or vice versa), he must notify and secure the consent of the Secretary.

Cash Basis

Cash basis taxpayers include income when it is *received,* and claim deductions when expenses are *paid.* A cash basis taxpayer can look to the doctrine of constructive receipt and the doctrine of cash equivalence to help determine when income is received. Most individuals start as cash basis taxpayers. There are three types of taxpayers that cannot use the cash basis:

(1) C corporations;

(2) partnerships with at least one C corporation partner; and

(3) tax shelters.

Similar definition of cash basis accounting is true for financial accounting purposes.

Accrual Basis

Accrual basis taxpayers include items when they are *earned* and claim deductions when expenses are *incurred.* An accrual basis taxpayer looks to the "all-events test" and "earlier-of test" to determine when income is earned. Under the all-events test, an accrual basis taxpayer generally must include income "for the taxable year when all the events have occurred that fix the right to receive income and the amount of the income can be determined with reasonable accuracy." Under the "earlier-of test", an accrual basis taxpayer receives income when (1) the required performance occurs, (2) payment therefor is due, or (3) payment therefor is made, whichever happens earliest.

Under the earlier of test outlined in Revenue Ruling 74-607, an accrual basis taxpayer may be treated, as a cash basis taxpayer, when payment is received before the required performance and before the payment is actually due. An accrual basis taxpayer generally can claim a deduction "in the taxable year in which all the events have occurred that establish the fact of the liability, the amount of the liability can be determined with reasonable accuracy, and economic performance has occurred with respect to the liability."

Similar definition of accrual basis accounting is true for financial accounting purposes, except that revenue can't be recognized until it's earned even if a cash payment has already been received.

History

Originally, federal law required all taxpayers to use the cash basis accounting. However, many businesses used the accrual basis, as most generally accepted accounting principles ("GAAP") were based thereon, and objected to the new law. Less than a year after the 1913 Revenue Act, the IRS allowed use of the accrual basis for deductions, then for income, and in 1916, Congress formally adopted the accrual basis accounting into U.S. tax law.

7

Analysis of Hospitality Budgeting

Policy Statement

The capital improvements program includes all capital projects, regardless of size, financed with state and University funds, and all departmentally funded projects exceeding $100,000 (see the Special Situations section for information on projects less than $100,000). The capital improvements program is an ongoing process that includes:

- Assessing capital needs, opportunities and resources
- Ensuring that potential projects conform with academic priorities & investment strategies
- Establishing priorities for project funding.

Provosts, Chancellors and Vice-Presidents submit their capital improvement needs for review by the Capital Improvements Advisory Committee which recommends systemwide priorities to the Senior Officers of the University. The President submits the capital budget to the Regents.

Exclusions

Purchases of free-standing instructional and research equipment, even those large enough to be categorized as a "capital expense", should be funded through the operating budget, and should not be submitted to the capital budgeting process. None of the funding sources available for allocation through the capital budget are available for free-standing equipment purchases.

Special Situations

Self-funded projects of less than $100,000 do not require individual approval by the Regents, and are, therefore, excluded from the capital budget process. These projects are handled as follows:

1. Projects are initiated by submitting a Form 1395 request to Capital Planning and Project Management with the dean's sign-off that the proposed project:
   * Conforms with academic priorities of the University
   * Has adequate funding identified
2. Projects are briefly reviewed to ensure that the proposed project:
   * Is within a facility worth investment
   * Will not significantly increase the cost of maintaining and operating the facility
   * Addresses code compliance issues
   * Causes no negative impact on adjacent space/facilities
   * Conforms with campus master planning principles
3. Projects that meet the preceding criteria will be scheduled for implementation immediately. Projects that do not appear to satisfy all of these criteria will be referred to the CIAC for review and recommendation, and to the Senior Officers for concurrence.
4. If during the planning and design stage the cost of a project increases beyond the $100,000 threshold, the project will be considered in the next capital budgeting cycle, or if the need is urgent, it may be handled as an amendment to the capital budget, requiring the review and recommendation of the CIAC, the concurrence of the Senior Officers, and the approval of the Regents.

Purchases of free-standing instructional and research equipment, even those large enough to be categorized as a "capital expense", should be funded through the operating budget, and should not be submitted to the capital budgeting process. None of the funding sources available for allocation through the capital budget are available for free-standing equipment purchases. However, if the equipment purchases require adjustments to building systems (examples: expanded electrical capacity, HVAC modification) or remodelling of space, those facility improvements should be submitted to the capital budgeting process in accordance with the definitions regarding project size and funding source contained in Section C. A department purchasing equipment which requires building adjustments must either invest departmental funds to achieve those modifications, or must request central funds through the capital budgeting process. If the purchase of equipment represents a high programmatic priority, the priorities for distributing capital resources may be influenced.

Reason for Policy

To assist the President in preparing the capital budget and capital improvements program. To facilitate informed investment decisions and promote effective management of existing capital assets.

Submitting a Project for the Capital Budget

Procedure

Types of Projects

All projects meeting the following definitions must be submitted to the capital budgeting process:

- Projects requesting central or state funding, regardless of size. Central and state funding sources include fire and life safety, ADA improved access, hazardous materials abatement, repair and replacement, program accommodation remodelling, internal loans, central reserves, University bonds and state bonds.
- Self-funded projects which exceed $100,000. Self-funding sources include departmental funds (O&M, ISO, ICR, gifts and grants) and fees collected by self-supported auxiliary services.

Academic units should submit only projects related to their programmatic needs. Projects that relate exclusively to fire and life safety, improved access, hazardous material abatement, or repair and replacement, should be referred to the units, listed below, that are responsible for addressing those needs.

Type of Improvement-Responsible Unit

Fire and Life Safety-University Building Official.

ADA access-Facilities Management TC Campus FM or Plant Services on other campuses. Hazardous material-Environmental Health and Safety / TC abatement Campus and air quality FM or Plant Services on other campuses.

Repair and replacement-Facilities Management on TC Campus FM or Plant Services on other campuses.

Submitting A Project

Submit capital projects to the capital budgeting process in the following manner:

- Departments identify a capital need, complete a project identification form, and submit it to the College or Resource Responsibility Center (RRC). Attach a copy of the project identification form.
- Colleges/RRCs review the requested capital improvement, assign a priority ranking to the request, and submit it to the Provost/Chancellor/Vice President.
- Provosts/Chancellors/Vice Presidents review the requested capital improvement, assign a preliminary priority ranking to the request, submit it to the Office of Budget and Finance, and present it to the Capital Improvements Advisory Committee (CIAC) budget hearings.

Project Identification Form

A project identification form must be submitted for all projects proposed for the period, including projects which were previously submitted and incorporated into the Capital Improvements Program. Each annual capital budget and capital improvements program is treated as a new undertaking, and confirmation of each project and its priority ranking is required if it is to remain in the capital improvements program. Project identification forms for projects included in the current capital improvements program are being returned to the Provosts, Chancellors, and Vice Presidents with instructions. Persons proposing those projects may obtain the forms from their Provost, Chancellor, or Vice President in order to improve the project information. If there are no changes, simply resubmit the sheets.

Project Identification Forms must be submitted by Oct. 31, 1996 CAPITAL BUDGET

To be considered for inclusion in the Capital Budget, the following conditions must be satisfied:

- Proposed construction projects must have a comprehensive cost estimate prepared by or under the direction of Capital Planning and Project Management. Proposed land or facility acquisitions must have an appraisal approved by the Real Estate Office.
- Proposed projects must have funding available, or have funding contingent upon a pending grant application or private gifts from an active fund raising campaign.

Unless both of these conditions are satisfied, the project will not be included in the Capital Budget, but will instead be placed in a future fiscal year of the capital improvements program.

Prior to Regents' approval of the capital budget, the Office of Budget and Finance will verify the availability of funding for projects which are dependent upon State and University funds. Departments and auxiliaries will be asked to verify the availability of funding for projects to be financed with departmental funds or with fees collected by self-supported auxiliaries by providing a CUFS account number, or by identifying a Foundation account, a grant application, or a fund raising effort.

Verification of funding must be received annually by April 1.

Projects must be identified during the annual budgeting process if they are to be considered for inclusion in the Capital Budget. Projects which are not identified at this time will be deferred to next year's budgeting cycle. Only in extraordinary circumstances will projects be considered as amendments to the approved capital budget during the course of the year. Budget amendments require special review and recommendation by the CIAC, concurrence by the Senior Officers, and approval by the Board of Regents. Implementation of a project cannot proceed until it has been included in the capital budget.

Equipment Purchases

Purchases of free-standing instructional and research equipment, even those large enough to be categorized as a "capital expense", should be funded through the operating budget, and should not be submitted to the capital budgeting process. None of the funding sources available for allocation through the capital budget are available for free-standing equipment purchases.

However, if the equipment purchases being considered will require adjustments to building systems (examples: expanded electrical capacity, HVAC modification) or remodelling of space, those facility improvements should be submitted to the capital budgeting process in accordance with the definitions regarding project size and funding source described at the beginning of this procedure. A department purchasing equipment which requires building adjustments must either invest departmental funds to achieve those modifications, or must request central funds through the capital budgeting process. If the purchase of equipment represents a high programmatic priority, the priorities for distributing capital resources may be influenced.

Discussion Issues and Derivations

Working Capital, Net Working Capital and Non-Cash Working Capital

Working capital is sometimes used to refer only to current assets, while net working capital is defined to be the difference between current assets and current liabilities. Non-cash working capital looks at the difference between non-cash current assets and current liabilities.

In investment analysis, increases in working capital are viewed as cash outflows, because cash tied up in working capital cannot be used elsewhere in the business and does not earn returns. It is the "does not earn returns" component of this definition that would lead us to look at non-cash working capital. Firms with significant cash balances today, especially in the US, earn market returns on their cash (by investing in at least T.Bills). Thus, the cash is productive and changes in the cash should not affect our cash flows.

To the degree that cash cannot be invested to earn market returns, and is needed for day-to-day operations, it is appropriate to look at changes in net working capital, with cash included.

Operating versus Capital Expenditures

Accountants draw a distinction between expenditures that yield benefits only in the immediate period or periods (such as labour and material for a manufacturing firm) and those that yield benefits over multiple periods (such as land, buildings and long-lived plant). The former are called operating expenses and are subtracted from revenues in computing the accounting income, while the latter are capital expenditures and are not subtracted from revenues in the period that they are made. Instead, the expenditure is spread over multiple periods and deducted as an expense in each period-these expenses are called depreciation (if the asset is a tangible asset like a building) or amortization (if the asset is an intangible asset like a patent or a trade mark).

While the capital expenditures made at the beginning of a project are often the largest and most prominent, many projects require capital expenditures during their lifetime. These capital expenditures will reduce the cash available in each of these periods.

Depreciation, Amortization and Other Non-cash Charges

The distinction that accountants draw between operating and capital expenses leads to a number of accounting expenses, such as depreciation and amortization, which are not cash expenses. These non-cash expenses, while depressing accounting income, do not reduce cash flows. In fact, they can have a significant positive impact on cash flows, if they affect the tax liability of the firm. Some non-cash charges reduce the taxable income and the taxes paid by a business. The most important of such charges is depreciation, which, while reducing taxable and net income, does not cause a cash outflow. Consequently, depreciation is added back to net income to arrive at the cash flows on a project. For projects that generate large depreciation charges, a significant portion of the cash flows can be attributed to the tax benefits of depreciation, which can be written as follows:

Tax Benefit of Depreciation = Depreciation * Marginal Tax Rate

While depreciation is similar to other tax deductible expenses in terms of the tax benefit it generates, its impact is more positive because it does not generate a concurrent cash outflow. Amortization is also a non-cash charge, but the tax effects of amortization can vary depending upon the nature of the amortization. Some amortization, such as the amortization of the price paid for a patent or a trade mark, are tax deductible and reduce both accounting income and taxes. Thus, they provide tax benefits similar to depreciation. Other amortization, such as the amortization of the premium paid on an acquisition (called goodwill), reduces accounting income but not taxable income. This amortization does not provide a tax benefit.

Capital Expenditures and Depreciation

In project analysis, it is important that assumptions about capital expenditures, depreciation and working capital be consistent. For instance,

- If the project is assumed to have a very long life or an infinite life, the firm will have to make much larger capital maintenance expenditure. As a simple rule of thumb, when projects have infinite life, the capital maintenance expenditures should approach depreciation. This will, if nothing else, ensure that the book value of the investment does not decline. More importantly, it is necessary to preserve the earning power of the assets
- For projects with shorter lives, it is possible that capital expenditures occur up front, and that depreciation in subsequent years is much greater than capital expenditure. The book value of the investment will decline over time to the salvage value.

ROC, Cost of Capital, NPV and EVA

Economic value added is a value enhancement concept that

has caught the attention of both firms interested in increasing their value and portfolio managers, looking for good investments. EVA is a measure of dollar surplus value created by a firm or project and is measured by doing the following:

Economic Value Added (EVA) = (Return on Capital-Cost of Capital) (Capital Invested)

where the return on capital is measured using "adjusted" operating income, where the adjustments eliminate items that are unrelated to existing investments, and the capital investment is based upon the book value of capital, but is designed to measure the capital invested in existing assets. Firms which have positive EVA are firms which are creating surplus value, and firms with negative EVA are destroying value.

In the context of investment analysis, the present value of the EVA created by a project should be equal to the net present value of the project.

ROE, Cost of Equity and Equity EVA

While EVA is usually calculated using total capital, it can be easily modified to be an equity measure:

Equity EVA = (Return on Equity-Cost of Equity) (Equity Invested in Project or Firm)

Again, a firm which earns a positive equity EVA is creating value for its stockholders while a firm with a negative equity EVA is destroying value for its stockholders.

Equity EVA may be the better way of thinking about value created for firms where capital is tough to measure (such as banks and insurance companies).

Equity Analysis versus Firm Analysis

An investment project can be analyzed in terms of all of the capital invested in the project (firm) or just from the perspective of the equity investors in the firm. If done consistently, cash flows to the firm discounted at the cost of capital or cash flows to equity discounted at the cost of equity, the two approaches should yield similar results if the following conditions hold:

a. The project is financed using the same mix of debt and equity as is used in the computation of the cost of capital.
b. The debt is assumed to have an interest rate equal to the pre-tax cost of debt

Currency Effects on Investment Analysis

One of the debates that analysts often engage in when doing investment analysis is whether the analysis should be done in one currency or another. Intuitively, an analysis of whether a project is a good or bad one should not depend upon what currency the analysis is done in. The important fact to keep in mind is that cash flows and the discount rate have to be estimated consistently. To convert the analysis from one currency to another would have required the following steps:

Step 1: Estimate the expected exchange rate for each period of the analysis.

While forward rates might be available for some currencies for a few periods, there are very few cases where forward rates will be available for the entire project life. To estimate the expected exchange rate, draw on the purchasing power parity theorem that argues that changes in exchange rates between two countries will reflect differences in inflation in those countries.

Step 2: Convert the expected cashflows from one currency to the other in future periods, using these exchange rates.

Step 3: Discount the expected cashflows at a discount rate, based upon the same currency.

Real versus Nominal Investment Analysis

Investment analyses can be done in terms of real or nominal cash flows. The discount rates have to be defined consistently-real for real cash flows and nominal for nominal cash flows. If done consistently, each analysis should yield the same net present value.

The choice between nominal and real cash flows therefore boils down to one of convenience. When inflation rates are low, it is better to do the analysis in nominal terms since taxes are based upon nominal income. When inflation rates are high and volatile, it is easier to do the analysis in real terms.

Given a choice, I would rather do the analysis in nominal terms, since taxes and financial statements are usually based upon nominal results.

Net Present Value, IRR or Modified IRR

For firms with no capital rationing constraints, net present value is clearly the choice that will maximize firm value the most. For firms with significant capital rationing constraints that will continue into the future, the IRR is likely to be the best solution. For firms with significant capital rationing constraints that will ease over time, the modified IRR is the best solution.

Corporate Strategy and Project Quality

In the process of analyzing new investments in the preceding chapters, we have contended that good projects have a positive net present value and earn an internal rate of return greater than the hurdle rate. While these criteria are certainly valid from a measurement standpoint, they do not address the deeper questions about good projects including the economic conditions that make for a "good" project and why it is that some firms have a more ready supply of "good" projects than others.

Implicit in the definition of a good project--one that earns a return that is greater than that earned on investments of equivalent risk--is the existence of super-normal returns to the business considering the project. In a competitive market for real investments, the existence of these excess returns should act as a magnet, attracting competitors to take on similar investments. In the process, the excess returns should dissipate over time; how quickly they dissipate will depend on the ease with which competition can enter the market and provide close substitutes and on the magnitude of any differential advantages that the business with the good projects might possess.

Take an extreme scenario, whereby the business with the good projects has no differential advantage in cost or product quality over its competitors, and new competitors can enter the market easily and at low cost to provide substitutes. In this case the super-normal returns on these projects should disappear very quickly. An integral basis for the existence of a "good" project is the creation and maintenance of barriers to new or existing competitors taking on equivalent or similar projects. These barriers can take different forms, including

a. *Economies of Scale*: Some projects might earn high returns only if they are done on a "large" scale, thus restricting competition from smaller companies. In such cases, large companies in this line of business may be able to continue to earn super-normal returns on their projects because smaller competitors will not be able to replicate them.

b. *Cost Advantages*: A business might work at establishing a cost advantage over its competitors, either by being more efficient or by taking advantage of arrangements that its competitors cannot use. For example, in the late 1980s, Southwest Airlines was able to establish a cost advantage over its larger competitors, such as American and United Airlines by using non-union employees, the company exploited this cost advantage to earn much higher returns.

c. *Capital Requirements*: Entry into some businesses might require such large investments that it discourages competitors from entering, even though projects in those businesses may earn above-market returns. For example, assume that Boeing is faced with a large number of high-return projects in the aerospace business. While this scenario would normally attract competitors, the huge initial investment needed to enter this business would enable Boeing to continue to earn these high returns.

d. *Product Differentiation*: Some businesses continue to earn excess returns by differentiating their products from those of their competitors, leading to either higher profit margins or higher sales. This differentiation can be created in a number of ways-through effective advertising and promotion (Coca Cola), technical expertise (Sony), better service (Nordstrom) and responsiveness to customer needs.

e. *Access to Distribution Channels*: Those firms that have much better access to the distribution channels for their products than their competitors are better able to earn excess returns. In some cases, the restricted access to outsiders is due to tradition or loyalty to existing competitors. In other cases, the firm may actually own the distribution channel, and competitors may not be able to develop their own distribution channels because the costs are prohibitive.

f. *Legal and Government Barriers*: In some cases, a firm may be able to exploit investment opportunities without worrying about competition because of restrictions on competitors from product patents the firm may own to government restrictions on competitive entry. These arise, for instance, when companies are allowed to patent products or services, and gain the exclusive right to provide them over the patent life.

Management and Project Quality

In the preceding section we examined some of the factors that determine the attractiveness of the projects a firm will face. While some factors, such as government restrictions on entry, may largely be out of the control of incumbent management, there are other factors that can clearly be influenced by management may largely be out of the control of incumbent management, there are other factors that can clearly be influenced by management. Considering each of the factors discussed above, for instance, we would argue that a good management team can increase both the number of and the returns on available projects by

- taking projects that exploit any economies of scale that the firm may possess; in addition, management can look for ways it can create economies of scale in the firm's existing operations.
- establishing and nurturing cost advantages over its competitors; some cost advantages may arise from labour negotiations, while others may result from long-term strategic decisions made by the firm. For instance, by owning and developing SABRE, the airline reservation system, American Airlines has been able to gain a cost advantage over its competitors.
- taking actions that increase the initial cost for new entrants into the business; one of the primary reasons Microsoft's

was able to dominate the computer software market in the early 1990s was its ability to increase the investment needed to develop and market software programs.

- increasing brand name recognition and value through advertising and by delivering superior products to customers; a good example is the success that Snapple experienced in the early 1990s in promoting and selling its iced tea beverages.
- nurturing markets in which the company's differential advantage is greatest, in terms of either cost of delivery or brand name value. In some cases, this will involve expanding into foreign markets, as both Levi Strauss and McDonalds did in the 1980s in order to exploit their higher brand name recognition in those markets. In other cases, this may require concentrating on segments of an existing market as The Gap did, when it opened its Banana Republic division, which sells upscale outdoor clothing.
- improving the firm's reputation for customer service and product delivery; this will enable the firm to increase both profits and returns. One of the primary factors behind Chrysler's financial recovery in the 1980s was the company's ability to establish a reputation for producing quality cars and minivans.
- developing distribution channels that are unique and cannot be easily accessed by competitors. Avon, for instance, employed large sales force to go door-to-door to reach consumers who could not be reached by other distribution channels.
- getting patents on products or technologies that keep out the competition and earn high returns; doing so may require large investments in research and development over time. It can be argued that Intel's success in the market for semiconductors can be traced to the strength of its research and development efforts and the patents it consequently obtained on advanced chips, such as the Pentium.

While the quality of management is typically related to the quality of projects a firm possesses, a good management team does not guarantee the existence of good projects. In fact, there is a rather large element of chance involved in the process; even the best laid plans of the management team to create project opportunities may come to naught if circumstances conspire against them-a recession may upend a retailer, or an oil price shock may cause an airline to lose money.

Working Capital Management

Defining Working Capital

The term working capital refers to the amount of capital which is readily available to an organisation. That is, working capital is the difference between resources in cash or readily convertible into cash (Current Assets) and organisational commitments for which cash will soon be required (Current Liabilities).

Current Assets are resources which are in cash or will soon be converted into cash in "the ordinary course of business".

Current Liabilities are commitments which will soon require cash settlement in "the ordinary course of business".

Thus:

WORKING CAPITAL = CURRENT ASSETS-CURRENT LIABILITIES

In a department's Statement of Financial Position, these components of working capital are reported under the following headings:

Current Assets

- Liquid Assets (cash and bank deposits)
- Inventory
- Debtors and Receivables

Current Liabilities

- Bank Overdraft
- Creditors and Payables
- Other Short Term Liabilities

The Importance of Good Working Capital Management

Working capital constitutes part of the Crown's investment in a department. Associated with this is an opportunity cost to the Crown. (Money invested in one area may "cost" opportunities for investment in other areas.) If a department is operating with more working capital than is necessary, this over-investment represents an unnecessary cost to the Crown. From a department's point of view, excess working capital means operating inefficiencies. In addition, unnecessary working capital increases the amount of the capital charge which departments are required to meet from 1 July 1991.

Approaches to Working Capital Management

The objective of working capital management is to maintain the optimum balance of each of the working capital components. This includes making sure that funds are held as cash in bank deposits for as long as and in the largest amounts possible, thereby maximising the interest earned. However, such cash may more appropriately be "invested" in other assets or in reducing other liabilities.

Working capital management takes place on two levels:

- Ratio analysis can be used to monitor overall trends in working capital and to identify areas requiring closer management.
- The individual components of working capital can be effectively managed by using various techniques and strategies.

When considering these techniques and strategies, departments need to recognise that each department has a unique mix of working capital components. The emphasis that needs to be placed on each component varies according to department. For example, some departments have significant inventory levels; others have little if any inventory. Furthermore, working capital management is not an end in itself. It is an integral part of the department's overall management. The needs of efficient working capital management must be considered in relation to other aspects of the department's financial and non-financial performance.

Financial Ratio Analysis

Financial ratio analysis calculates and compares various ratios of amounts and balances taken from the financial statements.

The main purposes of working capital ratio analysis are:

- to indicate working capital management performance; and
- to assist in identifying areas requiring closer management.

Three key points need to be taken into account when analyzing financial ratios:

- The results are based on highly summarised information. Consequently, situations which require control might not be apparent, or situations which do not warrant significant effort might be unnecessarily highlighted;
- Different departments face very different situations. Comparisons between them, or with global "ideal" ratio values, can be misleading;
- Ratio analysis is somewhat one-sided; favourable results mean little, whereas unfavourable results are usually significant.

However, financial ratio analysis is valuable because it raises questions and indicates directions for more detailed investigation.

The following ratios are of interest to those managing working capital:

- working capital ratio;
- liquid interval measure;
- stock turnover;
- debtors ratio;
- creditors ratio.

Working Capital Ratio

Current Assets divided by Current Liabilities

The working capital ratio (or current ratio) attempts to measure the level of liquidity, that is, the level of safety provided by the excess of current assets over current liabilities. The "quick ratio" a derivative, excludes inventories from the current assets, considering only those assets most swiftly realisable. There are also other possible refinements.

There is no particular benchmark value or range that can be recommended as suitable for all government departments. However, if a department tracks its own working capital ratio over a period of time, the trends-the way in which the liquidity is changing-will become apparent.

Liquid Interval Measure

Liquid Assets divided by Average Operating Expenses

This is another measure of liquidity. It looks at the number of days that liquid assets (for example, inventory) could service daily operating expenses (including salaries).

Stock Turnover

Cost of Sales divided by Average Stock Level

This ratio applies only to finished goods. It indicates the speed with which inventory is sold-or, to look at it from the other angle, how long inventory items remain on the shelves. It can be used for the inventory balance as a whole, for classes of inventory, or for individual inventory items.

The figure produced by the stock turnover ratio is not important in itself, but the trend over time is a good indicator of the validity of changes in inventory policies.

In general, a higher turnover ratio indicates that a lower level of investment is required to serve the department.

Most departments do not hold significant inventories of finished goods, so this ratio will have only limited relevance.

Debtor Ratio

There is a close relationship between debtors and credit sales to third parties (that is, sales other than to the Crown). If sales increase, debtors will increase, and conversely, if sales decrease debtors will decrease.

The best way to explain this relationship is to express it as the number of days that credit sales are carried on the books:

Credit Sales per Period x Days per Period

Average Debtors: Where trading terms are 30 days net cash, and customers buy from day-to-day during the 30 day period and pay 30 days after a statement is rendered, a collection period of 45 days (the average between 30 and 60 days) would be satisfactory.

If the average collection period extends beyond 60 days, debtors are holding cash that should have flowed into the department. This means that the department is unable to satisfy pressing liabilities or to invest that cash.

The debtor ratio does not solve the collection problem, but it acts as an indicator that an adverse trend is developing. Remedial action can then be instigated.

Creditor Ratio

This ratio is much the same as the debtor ratio. It expresses the relationship between credit purchases and the liability to creditors. It can be stated as the number of days that credit purchases are carried on the books.

Credit Purchases per Period × Days per Period

Average Creditors: Note that non-credit purchases (such as salaries) and non-cash expenses (such as depreciation) need to be excluded from "credit purchases" and any provisions need to be excluded from "creditors".

There is no need to pay creditors before payment is due. The department's objective should be to make effective use of this source of free credit, while maintaining a good relationship with creditors.

As with debtors, if a department has been granted credit terms of 30 days net cash, credit purchases should not be carried on the books for more than an average of 45 days. If payment is withheld for 60 days or more it is likely that creditors will become impatient and impose stricter and less convenient trading terms-for example, "cash on delivery".

The Public Finance Act 1989 (section 49) places a legal constraint on the amount of credit allowed to a department. It restricts to a maximum of 90 days the purchase of goods and services through the use of a credit card or suppliers' credit.

Specific Strategies

Inventories

Inventories are lists of stocks-raw materials, work in progress or finished goods-waiting to be consumed in production or to be sold.

The total balance of inventory is the sum of the value of each individual stock line. Stock records are needed:

- to provide an account of activity within each stock line;
- as evidence to support the balances used in financial reports.

A department also needs a system of internal controls to efficiently manage stocks and to ensure that stock records provide reliable information.

Departmental financial reports show only the total inventory balance. Analysts from outside the department can examine this balance by using ratio analysis or other techniques. However, this gives only a limited assessment of inventory management and is not adequate for internal management. Good financial management necessitates the careful analysis of individual inventory lines.

Inventory management is an important aspect of working capital management because inventories themselves do not earn any revenue. Holding either too little or too much inventory incurs costs.

Costs of carrying too much inventory are:

- opportunity cost of foregone interest;
- warehousing costs;
- damage and pilferage;
- obsolescence;
- insurance.

Costs of carrying too little inventory are:

- stockout costs:
    * lost sales;
    * delayed service.
- ordering costs:
    * freight;
    * order administration;
    * loss of quantity discounts.

Carrying costs can be minimised by making frequent small orders but this increases ordering costs and the risk of stock-outs. Risk of stock-outs can be reduced by carrying "safety stocks" (at a cost) and re-ordering ahead of time.

The best ordering strategy requires balancing the various cost factors to ensure the department incurs minimum inventory costs. The optimum inventory position is known as the Economic Reorder Quantity (ERQ).

There are a number of mathematical models (of varying complexity) for calculating ERQ. (Any standard accounting text will provide examples of these).

Analytical review of inventories can help to identify areas where inventory management can be improved. Slow moving items, continual stockouts, obsolescence, stock reconciliation problems and excess spoilage are signals that stock lines need closer analysis and control.

However, it is important to keep an overall perspective. It is not cost-effective to closely manage a large number of low value inventory lines, nor is it necessary. A usual feature of inventories is that a small number of high value lines account for a large proportion of inventory value.

The "80/20" rule (PARETO) predicts that 80% of the total value of inventory is represented by only 20% of the number of inventory items. Those high value lines need reasonably close management. The remaining 80% of inventory lines can be managed using "broad-brush" strategies.

The overall management philosophy of an organisation can affect the way in which inventory is managed.

For example, "Just In Time" (JIT) production management organises production so that finished goods are not produced until the customer needs them (minimising finished goods carrying costs), and raw materials are not accepted from suppliers until they are needed. (Large organisations have the power to insist that suppliers hold stocks of raw materials and thereby pass the carrying cost back to the supplier).

Thus, JIT inventory strategies reduce bottlenecks and stock holding costs.

In summary:

- There is a trade-off to be made between carrying costs, ordering costs, and stockout costs. This is represented in the Economic Reorder Quantity (ERQ) model.
- Inventories should be managed on a line-by-line basis using the 80/20 rule.
- Analytical review can help to focus attention on critical areas.
- Inventory management is part of the overall management strategy.

Debtors

Debtors (Accounts Receivable) are customers who have not yet made payment for goods or services which the department has provided. The objective of debtor management is to minimise the time-lapse between completion of sales and receipt of payment. The costs of having debtors are:

- opportunity costs (cash is not available for other purposes);
- bad debts.

Debtor management includes both pre-sale and debt collection strategies.

Pre-sale strategies include:

- offering cash discounts for early payment and/or imposing penalties for late payment;

- agreeing payment terms in advance;
- requiring cash before delivery;
- setting credit limits;
- setting criteria for obtaining credit;
- billing as early as possible;
- requiring deposits and/or progress payments.

Post-sale strategies include:

- Placing the responsibility for collecting the debt upon the center that made the sale;
- Identifying long overdue balances and doubtful debts by regular analytical reviews;
- Having an established procedure for late collections, such as
    * a reminder;
    * a letter;
    * cancellation of further credit;
    * telephone calls;
    * use of a collection agency;
    * legal action.

Creditors

Creditors (Accounts Payable) are suppliers whose invoices for goods or services have been processed but who have not yet been paid. Organisations often regard the amount owing to creditors as a source of free credit. However, creditor administration systems are expensive and time-consuming to run. The overriding concern in this area should be to minimise costs with simple procedures.

While it is unnecessary to pay accounts before they fall due, it is usually not worthwhile to delay all payments until the latest possible date., Regular weekly or fortnightly payment of all due accounts is the simplest technique for creditor management.

Electronic payments (direct credits) are cheaper than cheque payments, considering that transaction fees and overheads more than balance the advantage of delayed presentation. Some suppliers are reluctant to receive payments by this method, but in view of the substantial cost advantage (and the advantages to the suppliers themselves) departments may wish to encourage suppliers to accept this option. However, electronic payments are likely to be used in conjunction with, rather than as a replacement for, cheque payments.

Cash and Bank

Good cash management can have a major impact on overall working capital management.

The key elements of cash management are:

- cash forecasting;
- balance management;
- administration;
- internal control.

Cash Forecasting: Good cash management requires regular forecasts. In order for these to be materially accurate, they must be based on information provided by those managers responsible for the amounts and timing of expenditure. Capital expenditure and operating expenditure must be taken into account. It is also necessary to collect information about impending cash transactions from other financial systems, such as creditors and payroll.

Balance Management: Those responsible for balance management must make decisions about how much cash should at any time be on call in the Departmental Bank Account and how much should be on term deposit at the various terms available.

There are various types of mathematical model that can be used. One type is analogous to the ERQ inventory model. Linear programming models have been developed for cash management, subject to certain constraints. There are also more sophisticated techniques.

Administration: Cash receipts should be processed and banked as quickly as possible because:

- They cannot earn interest or reduce overdraft until they are banked;

- Information about the existence and amounts of cash receipts is usually not available until they are processed.

Where possible, cash floats (mainly petty cash and advances) should be avoided. If, on review, the only reason that can be put forward for their existence is that "we've always had them", they should be discontinued. There may be situations where they are useful, however. For example, it may be desirable for peripheral parts of departments to meet urgent local needs from cash floats rather than local bank accounts.

Internal Control: Cash and cash management is part of a department's overall internal control system. The main internal cash control is invariably the bank reconciliation. This provides assurance that the cash balances recorded in the accounting systems are consistent with the actual bank balances. It requires regular clearing of reconciling items.

Other Components

Working capital, defined as the difference between current assets and current liabilities, may also include the following factors:

- prepayments to creditors;
- current portions of long-term liabilities;
- revenue received before it has been earned;
- provisions.

However, decisions on working capital management usually exclude these factors, so they have not been included in this booklet.

Summary

Good management of working capital is part of good financial management. Effective use of working capital will contribute to the operational efficiency of a department; optimum use will help to generate maximum returns. Ratio analysis can be used to identify working capital areas which require closer management. Various techniques and strategies are available for managing specific working capital items. Debtors, creditors, cash and in some cases inventories are the areas most likely to be relevant to departments.

Bibliography

Douglas C: *Practical Tourism Forecasting,* Oxford, Butterworth Heinemann, 1996.

Foster, Douglas: *Travel and Tourism Management,* London, Macmillan Educational, 1985.

Frechtling, Douglas C: *Practical Tourism Forecasting,* Oxford, Butterworth Heinemann, 1996.

Ghimire, Krishna: *The Native Tourist*: Mass Tourism within Developing Regions, London, Earthscan, 2001.

Hoffman, Edward: *Project Management Success Stories: Lessons of Project Leaders,* New York, John Wiley & Son, 2000.

Horner, S. and Swarbrooke, J.: *Marketing Tourism, Hospitality and Leisure in Europe,* London, International Thomson Business Press, 1996.

Ireland, Lewis: *Quality Management for Projects and Programs,* Upper Darby, PMI, 1991.

Jakle, John: *Tourist, The: Travel in Twentieth Century North America,* University of North Nebraska, 1985.

Jennings, Gayle: *Tourism Research,* Chichester, Wiley, 2001.

Judi Radice: *Restaurant & Food Graphics,* Glen Cove, PBC International, 1994.

Karski, A: *Urban Tourism* - A Key to Urban Regeneration?, 1990.

Kharbanda, O. and E. Stallworthy: *Waste Management Towards a Sustainable Society,* Auburn House, New York, 1990.

Klein, S. : *Information & Communication Technologies in Tourism,* Springer-Verlag, Wien-New York, 2000.

Kotler, Philip et al: *Marketing Places: Attracting Investment, Industry & Tourism etc,* New York, free press, 1993.

Labarge, Margaret Wade: *Medieval Travellers: The Rich and Restless*, London, Hamish Hamilton, 1982.

Lawrence, E. : *Technology of internet business*, Wiley, Australia, 2002.

Laws, Eric: *Tourist Destination Management: Issues, Analysis & Policies*, London, Routledge, 1995.

Leivadi, S: *Sociology of Tourism, The: Theoretical And Empirical Investigations*, London, Retailed, 1996.

Lewis, Robert C.: *Cases in Hospitality Marketing and Management*, New York, John Wiley, 1997.

Lucas, Rosemary E.: *Managing Employee Relations in the Hotel and Catering Industry*, London, Cassell, 1995.

Marcussen, Carl H. : *Internet Distribution of European Travel and Tourism Services*, Research Centre of Bornholm, Denmark, 1999.

Marjorie, E.: *Careers in Travel, Tourism, and Hospitality*, Lincolnwood, VGM Career Horizons, 1997.

Morrell, J. : *Employment in Tourism*, London: British Tourist Authority, 1985.

Norman G.: *Hotel, Restaurant, and Travel Law: A Preventive Approach*, Albany, Delmar Publishers, 1993.

Peter J.: *College & University Foodservice Management Standards*, Westport, AVI Pub. Company, 1985.

Peters, M: *International Tourism*, London, Hutchinson, 1969.

Phipps, A: *Tourism and Intercultural Exchange: Why Tourism Matters*, Clevedon, Channel View, 2005.

Prentice, R: *Conceptualising The Experiences of Heritage Tourists*, 1997.

Rocco, M.: *An Introduction to Hospitality Today*, Orlando, Educational Institute, 1998.

Rosenzweig, J. E.: *Organisation and Management*, New York, McGraw Hill International, 1963.

Rue, Nancy N.: *Choosing a Career in Hotels, Motels, and Resorts*, New York, Rosen Pub. Group, 1997.

Schwaninger, M: *Trends in Leisure and Tourism for 2000 - 2010,* Prentice Hall, 1989.

Sharma Sunil : *Planning and Development of Tourism and Hospitality,* Rajat Pub, Delhi, 2007..

Slinn, Judy A: *Tourism: Management of Facilities,* London, Pitman: M & E, 1993.

Stallworthy, E.: *Waste Management Towards a Sustainable Society,* Auburn House, New York, 1990.

Swarbrooke, J.: *Marketing Tourism, Hospitality and Leisure in Europe,* London, International Thomson Business Press, 1996.

Timothy R.: *Cases in Hospitality Management: A Critical Incident Approach,* New York, Wiley, 1995.

Var, Turgut: *Tourism Planning,* London, Retailed, 2002.

Index

❑❑❑